More praise for *Standing in the Fire*

"Larry Dressler helps us to increase our capacities and practices to lead meetings that are often a test by fire, enabling us to feel the burn and not be burned out but rather be inspired to achieve more effective outcomes."
—Susan A. Bouchard, Senior Business Development Manager, Cisco Systems Inc., and author of *Enterprise Web 2.0 Fundamentals*

"Clear and potent, *Standing in the Fire* presents a transformed way of being for conveners and facilitators of conflictual meetings. Learning to appreciate and apply its principles and practices sets the stage for breakthrough possibilities for today's challenged leaders."
—Juanita Brown and David Isaacs, coauthors of *The World Café*

"Dressler offers a new perspective and a new set of tools to help channel fire into transformative outcomes. This is a must-read for anyone who must navigate through a sea of emotionally charged issues."
—Russell Coff, Associate Professor of Organization and Management, Emory University

"Today's business leaders have to practice the capacity to stand with conflict and confusion in the kinds of challenges they face. Larry Dressler's fine book gives everyone a framework to understand what's going on in these moments and the skills to stand in a powerful combination of strength and sensitivity."
—Christina Baldwin and Ann Linnea, coauthors of *The Circle Way*

"Larry Dressler writes with clarity and deep understanding. He provides an accessible perspective and practical wisdom for moving past the urge to react when things go scarily out of control."
—Saul Eisen, PhD, Program Coordinator, Organization Development Program, Sonoma State University

"*Standing in the Fire* affirmed for me that learning to lead others through uncertainty and conflict is, at its heart, a spiritual journey. Larry Dressler has written another provocative and inspiring book that I'll use and share with colleagues for many years to come."
—Steve Fox, Executive Vice President, Central Conference of American Rabbis

"The more complex the challenges, the more likely the solutions involve passing through the flames of change. Offering compelling wisdom from the inside out, *Standing in the Fire* equips you to support groups in making it through. Step in with both feet!"
—Peggy Holman, coauthor and coeditor, *The Change Handbook*

STANDING
IN THE FIRE

Standing in the Fire

LEADING HIGH-HEAT

MEETINGS WITH CALM,

CLARITY, AND COURAGE

Larry Dressler

BK̄

Berrett–Koehler Publishers, Inc.
a BK Business book

Berrett-Koehler Publishers, Inc.
1333 Broadway, Suite 1000
Oakland, CA 94612-1921
Tel: (510) 817-2277   Fax: (510) 817-2278   www.bkconnection.com

ORDERING INFORMATION

Quantity sales. Special discounts are available on quantity purchases by corporations, associations, and others. For details, contact the "Special Sales Department" at the Berrett-Koehler address above.

Individual sales. Berrett-Koehler publications are available through most bookstores. They can also be ordered directly from Berrett-Koehler: Tel: (800) 929-2929; Fax: (802) 864-7626; www.bkconnection.com

Orders for college textbook/course adoption use. Please contact Berrett-Koehler: Tel: (800) 929-2929; Fax: (802) 864-7626.

Distributed to the U.S. trade and internationally by Penguin Random House Publisher Services.

Berrett-Koehler and the BK logo are registered trademarks of Berrett-Koehler Publishers, Inc.

Printed in the United States of America

Berrett-Koehler books are printed on long-lasting acid-free paper. When it is available, we choose paper that has been manufactured by environmentally responsible processes. These may include using trees grown in sustainable forests, incorporating recycled paper, minimizing chlorine in bleaching, or recycling the energy produced at the paper mill.

Library of Congress Cataloging-in-Publication Data
Dressler, Larry, 1961–
  Standing in the fire : leading high-heat meetings with calm, clarity, and courage / Larry Dressler.—1st ed.
     p.   cm.
  Includes bibliographical references and index.
  ISBN 978-1-57675-970-7 (pbk. : alk. paper)
  1. Business meetings. 2. Management. I. Title.
  HF5734.5.D74 2010
  658.4'56—dc22   2009048846

First Edition
24 23 22 21 20 19   10 9 8 7 6

Designed and produced by Seventeenth Street Studios
Copy editing by Karen Seriguchi
Cover designed by Mark van Bronkhorst, MVB Design
Cover image: © Claudia Dewald / iStockphoto
Author photo: Michael Brooks

CONTENTS

FOREWORD

ON AUGUST 5, 1949, AT MANN Gulch, Montana, Wagner Dodge entered history by standing in the fire. A veteran smoke jumper, Dodge parachuted into Mann Gulch with his crew to put out a ground fire that had started from a bolt of lightning. When they boarded the C-47 military transport in Missoula, the fire was small. But, by 4:10 p.m., when they parachuted in and arrived near the gulch, the fire was out of control.

Dodge and his men set up across the gulch so that the Missouri River and a large stand of pines separated them from the fire. The terrain made it difficult to see the fire's path, and when the group crested a ridge, they saw that the fire had crossed the gulch and was only a few hundred yards away. Dodge yelled to his men to retreat, and they began running up the steep canyon walls. But the fire was moving toward them at thirty miles an hour and gaining speed. Dodge realized that he and his men would soon be suffocated or burned to death trying to outrun it. So he stopped running.

Managing his fear of imminent death, Dodge invented a solution. Facing the blaze, he lit a ring of fire around himself. It quickly created a patch of burned earth, over which he hoped the blaze would "jump." Dodge yelled for his men to lie down with him in the newly burned patch, but the men kept running, either because they couldn't hear him or didn't listen. The fire swept over them. Thirteen men were left dead. Wagner Dodge emerged from the fire practically unscathed.

We who work with groups are often figuratively, rather than literally, standing in the fire. Our fires start when challenging issues flare up in groups and mix with fuel from our own issues. Still, the lessons learned from the Mann Gulch fire ring true for us as well:

- You never know when a fire will ignite or shift direction.

- What has worked for you in the past may not work now. Successfully standing in the fire often means inventing new tools and techniques in the moment.

- Fire can even be your friend if you respect it and know how to use it.

- Ultimately, successfully standing in the fire is about developing a mindset—a way of thinking and feeling—that enables you to be calm, curious, courageous, compassionate, and flexible. Without this mindset, you are lost.

In *Standing in the Fire*, Larry Dressler addresses a critical issue for those of us who help groups. Although it is important to have tools and techniques in our kit, they have little value if our thoughts and feelings undermine our ability to use them. Each of us faces issues that make us less effective at helping others become more effective. These issues distort our ability to see clearly and act in service to the group. Some of us get defensive when people with power challenge us; some of us get angry when others don't take initiative or responsibility; some of us want to be liked so much that we do things for the group that we shouldn't. I could go on, but I assume you get the point. For the past thirty years I have helped OD and HR professionals, facilitators, and organizational leaders get better results and build better relationships. To help them achieve these results, nothing has been more important than helping them address the thoughts and feelings that undermine their effectiveness. Like my clients and my colleagues, I have faced these issues as well as others. And I am still learning.

Learning to stand in the fire means doing internal work. It is a discipline and a journey. The path differs for each of us, and there is more than one way to stand effectively. We need a guide to help us explore when and how we lose our balance, help us learn how to regain it, and help us develop ways of showing up with groups so we are more likely to remain calm, curious, compassionate, and courageous. That guide is what *Standing in the Fire* delivers.

Doing this work is not only for helping others; it is for you. When you increase your ability to stand in the fire, you think and act authentically with compassion for others and yourself. You spend less time worrying about what might happen, what is happening, or what will happen. You feel less angry, less guilty, and less disappointed. You have more energy to do your work, and you enjoy it more. In short, you increase your mental health. Ultimately, this is a gift to yourself.

Larry is an ideal guide to help us on this journey. He is the real deal. I first met Larry several years ago, when he was presenting a short workshop on "Standing in the Fire" to a conference of professional facilitators. When I walked into the room, Larry introduced himself. When I introduced myself, he said something like, "I'm really glad you're here; I really value your work, and your books have had a big influence on me.

I'm also feeling anxious knowing you're in the session." What struck me was how transparent and calm Larry seemed and how willing he was to be vulnerable with me. We had met less than a minute ago and he was able to identify how he was feeling toward me and articulate it in a way that quickly built a relationship between us. A little later I realized that, in his introduction, he had practiced what he was teaching us in the session. I thought to myself, "This is a guy I want to learn from." Since that day, Larry and I have been colleagues, meeting virtually and regularly to learn with and from each other.

Learning to stand in the fire is personal work, and Larry is a personal guide. To help us on our journey, he shares his own journey with us. He shows us how to challenge ourselves by showing how he has challenged himself. He shows us how to laugh at ourselves by laughing at himself. And he shows us how to be compassionate with ourselves by being compassionate with himself. In sum, he helps us safely navigate challenging terrain and arrive at a better place. Enjoy the journey.

—Roger Schwarz
Author of *The Skilled Facilitator:*
A Comprehensive Resource for Consultants, Facilitators,
Managers, Trainers, and Coaches

PREFACE

WE WHO DESIGN AND FACILITATE meetings for a living tend to see our work in two dimensions: (1) the *what*—the content of the gatherings we facilitate, which includes the purpose, questions, challenges, and possibilities that matter most to the people in the groups we serve; and (2) the *how*—the structures, methods, skills, and techniques we use to help a group mobilize its collective energy, insights, and commitment to action. It's in this second dimension that our special expertise really comes into play. Our ability to assist groups with the *how* of complex, emotional, important conversations is what makes us uniquely helpful in the world of high-stakes meetings.

Whether we admit it or not, the conventional wisdom of many people who do this kind of work is *If I can only learn a few more methods, I'll be able to handle any group situation!* And so we keep investing time and money in books, workshops, and conferences that focus exclusively on *how*. We collect tools and methods as if they were marbles. And even with a full bag of techniques, we are surprised when the messiness of a meeting pulls us into feeling anxious, defensive, and unable to think clearly or to draw effectively on our accumulated knowledge and skills.

Experienced facilitators, consultants, community activists, and organizational leaders often find themselves "standing in the fire"— working in situations where group members are polarized, angry, fearful, and confused. In these difficult meetings it's rarely enough to have a solid understanding of what is being said or how to use group intervention methods. In these high-heat situations, the truly master-ful change agents draw on something else—something that most lead-ers have invested little time and effort to cultivate. That something is *who* we are being while we are working with the group. Beyond our vast inventory of theories and techniques is something I've come to believe is the difference between competence and true mastery. It is the convener's *way of being*—an attitudinal, emotional, physical, and even spiritual presence. It is a specific kind of presence that others experience as fully engaged, open, authentic, relaxed, and grounded in purpose.

This book does not contain a single tip or technique on what to do to others during a high-heat meeting. It offers no framework or inter-vention for getting a group or individual group members from point A to point B. This book offers instead a set of internal, self-directed principles and practices that enable you to be a non-anxious, grounded presence in situations where others are feeling hopeless, agitated, angry, or confused.

The premise of *Standing in the Fire* is that what (knowledge) and how (methods, techniques, interventions) are only as effective as who is delivering them. If who we are in any given moment is anxious or defensive, our attempts to be in service to the group will at best fall flat and, at worse, amplify the group's distress.

"Who we are" doesn't refer to charisma or enthusiasm. It doesn't mean we are numb to the emotion swirling around the room. It means we show up with integrity and choose the kind of presence we need to embody from one moment to the next.

This book is about pursuing the possibility that each of us can exponentially increase the power of our methods and the wisdom of our choices when we have greater self-awareness about who we are being as we face the heat of group fire.

What Influences Have Shaped My Thinking?

Since my elementary school days in Southern California, when I tried to make my way safely through school hallways dominated by bullies and gang members, I've been holding different versions of the same question: *What are the human qualities that enable one to bring peace, clarity, and hopefulness into a situation that is filled with conflict, uncertainty, and despair?* For most of my adult life I've made my livelihood as an organizational development consultant and process facilitator, which has been in large part a vehicle for me to explore this question on both an academic and a personal level.

If I bring a bias to my work and to the writing of this book, it is a belief that no single school of thought or discipline has a monopoly on useful wisdom. The insights and practices offered here are drawn from conventional and unconventional sources alike, including psychology, complexity theory, neurobiology, Eastern and Western spiritual traditions, the performing arts, and nature. Any idea or practice in these pages is here because of one reason—it offers a useful stepping-stone toward making a positive, even transformational, contribution in the midst of challenging human interactions.

Who Should Read This Book?

Since the earliest human societies, leadership has involved the act of convening—bringing diverse individuals together to pursue a common purpose. Whether you think of yourself as a process facilitator, executive leader, organizational development consultant, mediator, clergy member, educator, community organizer, or change agent, your job involves skillfully convening others in a way that helps them discover and mobilize their shared wisdom and energy. If the word *convening* describes a significant part of your work, this book was written for you. Your capacity to bring into the room a clear, calm, compassionate presence is essential to your effectiveness as a convener, regardless of your specific role or title.

What's Ahead?

Imagine basking in the personal insights and stories of forty of the most experienced conveners you know—a group of people who live on five continents and whose accumulated experience totals over nine hundred years! During the research for this book, my colleague Erica Peng and I had the pleasure of interviewing a remarkable mix of leaders, conveners, change agents, and facilitators—people who know group fire intimately. They work with groups that are tackling some of the most difficult challenges around the world: global hunger, AIDS, the environmental crisis, peace, and postwar reconciliation. The names of these esteemed teachers and friends, many of whom will be recognizable to you as thought leaders in their own right, appear in the acknowledgments. You will see their wisdom throughout these pages.

PART I: THE FIRE

This book is organized into three parts. Part I describes the nature of group fire and what it takes to be a change agent who works in high-heat situations. The introduction highlights the key propositions and insights of the book, providing an overview of what follows. Chapter 1, "Fire for Better or Worse," explores the creative and destructive potential of emotional intensity and discord in groups. It describes various facets of group fire as well as how and why change agents often get swept away in their own self-inflicted fires. Chapter 2, "We Are Fire Tenders," describes how people who convene meetings can use the fullness of their presence to help the group hold a clear and intentional space for strong emotions, conflict, and complexity as its members work to discover new insights and common ground.

PART II: SIX WAYS OF STANDING

The second section of the book describes the mental, emotional, and physical ways of being that enable us to be effective fire tenders. Chapter 3, "Stand with Self-Awareness," describes how we can become skilled observers of our own thoughts and emotions in order to minimize defensive reactions and make more deliberate choices in high-heat situations. Chapter 4, "Stand in the Here and Now," offers a set of capacities that enable us to stay in the present moment instead of getting caught up in regrets about the past or predictions about the future. In chapter 5, "Stand with an Open Mind," we examine the ways in which we can stay grounded in curiosity and inquiry, even in the face of our own impulsive judgments about what is happening in a meeting. Chapter 6, "Know What You Stand For," is about learning to ground ourselves in our purpose, core principles, and clear commitment to be of service to the group with which we are working. Chapter 7, "Dance with Surprises," explores the capacities we must cultivate in ourselves in order to overcome our need for certainty and control. These capacities enable us to move creatively and flexibly as unexpected events unfold in our meetings. Chapter 8, "Stand with Compassion," describes the ways in which we can lose our empathy for group members when we are in a reactive mode. The capacities described in this chapter enable us to extend a more open heart and greater dignity toward ourselves and others.

PART III: PRACTICES

The third section of the book offers a wide variety of personal practices to help us cultivate the inner capacities described in part II. Chapter 9, "Cultivate Everyday Readiness," offers practices that facilitators and change agents can use on an ongoing basis to develop greater awareness and to make more deliberate choices in the fire. In Chapter 10, "Prepare to Lead," we examine what facilitators can do before a meeting. These practices help to connect us with the physical space, our inner state, our intention, the meeting participants. Chapter 11, "Face the Fire," offers a set of practices that can be used during a meeting to shift ourselves into a more intentional state after we notice an emotional hot button has been pushed. Chapter 12, "Reflect and Renew," contains practices that we can use after our meeting has concluded. These practices are aimed at fostering continuous learning as well as physical, mental, emotional, and spiritual regeneration.

Each chapter concludes with a set of Questions for Reflection, and chapters 1 through 8 offer an exercise called Try This. These exploratory questions and self-guided exercises are designed to move your learning beyond intellectual understanding and toward practical, everyday application.

Conveners of high-stakes gatherings think a lot about the exterior landscapes of meetings. We have developed ways to structure group processes. We have created techniques for helpfully intervening. We sometimes operate as if what happens in the room is all there is. But as Parker Palmer wrote, "We are constantly engaged in a seamless exchange between whatever is 'out there' and whatever is 'in here' co-creating reality for better or for worse."[1] This book deals with the next frontier of facilitator learning—developing what's "in here" so that we can partner well with what's "out there." The goal of this inner journey is to ensure that whoever shows up as convener, leader, and co-creator of high-heat conversations brings the fullness of his or her personal resources into the infinitely creative and often challenging circle of human interaction.

I hope that *Standing in the Fire* becomes one of those books in your life whose pages you dog-ear and fill with marginal notes. Use this book as a way to affirm your natural gifts and to explore the personal capacities you aspire to develop. As you read, take the time to reflect a bit on what these lessons might mean for you, and the mark you want to make as a leader. And know that even as I write these words, I am on this learning journey with you. The most liberating aspect about this book is that it contains not one tip about how to change anyone else. This is a book for and about you.

THE POWER
OF FIRE

CAN YOU REMEMBER THE MOST intense high-heat moment you've faced working with a group? One of my most memorable moments happened fairly early in my career, but I remember it vividly. Catherine, my consulting partner at the time, and I were working with a group of federal law enforcement officers. A conflict between two divisions of the agency had escalated over several months, and just prior to our first meeting, a few employees were caught vandalizing the vehicles of their co-workers by scratching the car doors with keys. People could hardly remember the origin of the conflict, but both factions believed they were in the right. The rift had taken on a life of its own and was now being played out in a cycle of revenge and retaliation.

At the first meeting everyone arrived on time, and as the officers sat down and positioned their chairs, the seating configuration started to look more and more like two circles. The geography of the conflict was clear from the outset, and the tension in the room was palpable. As they waited for the meeting to begin, people sat with crossed arms and legs, hardly able to look at members of the other group. Just as we were about to begin, Catherine and I noticed that everyone was wearing a gun.

All I could think about in that moment was the twenty or so guns strapped to people who were really angry at each other. My heart was beating fast, and my face felt flushed. I remember looking toward the exit for reassurance. In that moment, I had no idea what to do or say, and Catherine looked only slightly more composed.

What Gets Ignited

It doesn't take firearms to remind us of our vulnerability when we step into the room as the convener of a high-stakes meeting. Sometimes it takes only a skeptically raised eyebrow from a powerful person in the room; other times, a realization that the group will run out of time before achieving its goal. What creates heat for each of us depends largely on our personal hot buttons.

When these buttons are pushed, two kinds of energy can be ignited. One kind of energy connects to an age-old human survival instinct, the *self-protective reaction*. It's habitual, often emotionally charged, and designed to bring us back to our comfort zone. The second kind of energy can be accessed only if we can ask ourselves, *Who do I want to be right now?* This question ignites the energy of *deliberate choice and wise action*. This book is about building our capacity to ignite the second energy, even when our fears and ego encourage us to do otherwise.

What Is the Who?

Staring into the heat of a challenging group dynamic, we instinctively want to do something. We attempt to find just the right intervention that will make things easier for the group or perhaps for us. With little awareness of our internal dialogue or our emotional state, we take action. And too often that action turns out to be either the wrong choice or a reasonable choice poorly executed. Too often, no action was needed at all. What was needed was a facilitative leader who could serve as a steady, impartial, purposeful presence in the room, holding the space of the conversation with good humor, resoluteness, and compassion.

Who we are in these moments of fire is in itself a powerful intervention. We do not need to be the picture of charisma or Zen-like detachment. Instead we need to stand in a way that has integrity for us and is in service to the group we are there to assist. Our power comes from the realization that we always have a choice about which *who* shows up.

IN SEARCH OF HOT SPOTS

Without passion, conviction, and yearning, there would be no human fire. And without fire, groups would produce very little of interest or positive impact. We need fire to progress, but we also need to help people channel its heat. That's the job of *fire tenders*—people who know how to bring out the life-generating, creative potential of group fire.

Cultivating the creative potential of fire is the only useful approach, because fire suppression doesn't work. Too many leaders and institutions avoid or stifle the critical conversations that need to happen, and the results are often disastrous. Many case studies have been written about Enron and its predominant culture, in which challenging the status quo or raising concerns was simply not acceptable. Dissent was discouraged in a wide variety of subtle and not-so-subtle ways. The policy of suppression ultimately led to the demise of the company. In order to create organizations and communities in which people feel safe speaking their truth, we need leaders who are both skillful at process and who possess the capacity to remain self-aware, open, and fluid even as others struggle with dissent, confusion, and fear.

Fire tenders are drawn to the hot spots of social existence because they know that where there is heat, there is the possibility of transformation. Though they seek out and cultivate heat with great skill, they know their most important tool is their interior self—their mindset, emotional state, and the way they occupy their bodies. They understand that no matter what is producing heat "out there" in the group, they control their own thermostat.

Standing in Service to the Group

Standing is a word with many meanings. When we say, "My decision stands," the decision remains valid or effective. When we say, "I can't stand it," we mean endure or tolerate. When we "stand up," we are rising to our feet or picking ourselves up. When we communicate "our stand" on an issue, the word refers to an attitude or outlook. "Standing in the fire" encompasses all those meanings. As leaders, we must remain effective in our facilitative roles. Often we need to endure situations we experience as uncomfortable. Inevitably we are knocked off balance by the intense energy of others and must pick ourselves up quickly and regain our equilibrium. When we stand as fire tenders, we are choosing a particular set of attitudes—a way of seeing what is happening and who we are in the moment.

This book explores six interrelated ways of standing in the fire. You will learn what it is like to stand with self-awareness, presence, receptivity, intention, fluidity, and compassion. For each of these ways of standing in the fire, this book describes the capacities you need to succeed.

A Lifetime of Practice

Masterful fire tenders have a set of personal practices aimed at cultivating self-awareness and effective action. These practices help us choose our way of standing when we face the fire. Every moment, whether inside or outside a meeting, is an opportunity to practice. We can develop ongoing practices that aid us in developing everyday readiness. We can engage in special practices for our arrival at meetings, and we can use practices that help us recover during a meeting when a hot button gets pushed. We need practices that help us to reflect and to renew ourselves after we have come through a human firestorm. Contrary to the popular saying, practice does not "make perfect." Instead, practice is where we can break through the illusions of perfectionism and control as we learn to become present to our own wisdom during moments in which others find it difficult to access theirs.

Inviting Fire

As we engage in practice and derive new insights from our experiences in groups, we come to realize that destructive fires like distraction, fear, and aggression are all self-inflicted. As we develop greater mastery, we learn to recognize dissent and confusion as old, familiar friends. We welcome inconvenient surprises as useful fuel, and we come to view group breakdowns as the natural precursor to breakthroughs.

The more we work with fire, the more we see it as a source of transformation not only for groups, but also for us as agents of change. Each time we invite dissent, possibility, suffering, passion, or confusion into the room, we must also invite that which is calm, clear, and courageous within us—our wisest, most centered self. Each time we accept this invitation, we honor a proposition as old as humankind's relationship with fire—that conversation and human connection will change this world for the better.

THE FIRE

The language of fire and heat has long been part of our way of describing social interaction. For example, we say, *The sparks were really flying! The exchange got quite heated. She made an inflammatory comment. He burnt his bridges when he left. She was in the hot seat.* When we bring people together to talk about what matters to them, fire is a given. Where there is passion, conviction, and diversity, you can bet there will be heat.

This section of the book describes the destructive and creative potential of group fire, the many forms that fire takes in social interactions, and the ways in which a facilitator or convener can get swept away in the heat of the moment. We will also explore who we need to be in order to help groups use their emotional energy productively to come through the inevitable periods of conflict, confusion, and despair.

It seems that meetings are becoming more and more combustible—emotionally intense, polarized, or complicated. In my experience, emotional intensity is more likely to occur under the following conditions:

- The outcome of the process is highly uncertain.

- The issue is complex and not fully understood.
- The group has a history of suffering and loss.
- Discussion of the issue has been suppressed in the past.
- Expression of emotion about the issue has also been suppressed.
- The stakes are high.
- Big power differentials exist among those who have a stake.
- The people involved are highly diverse (in personality, culture, etc.).
- People have strong positions and resist seeing alternative points of view.
- The group is physically, mentally, or emotionally fatigued.
- People have hidden agendas and use manipulative tactics.

If you look at this list and think, "More and more of my meetings are held under these conditions," take that as confirmation that you are working in a highly combustible human landscape. It's imperative that you understand this landscape and your role in it.

■

FIRE FOR BETTER OR WORSE

It was a familiar feeling—tightness in my chest and the back of my neck. This told me it was time to breathe, trust, let go of attachment to outcome, listen deeply to what was going on, and test things that might or might not go well.

—Gibran Rivera

Senior Associate,

Interaction Institute for Social Change

GROUP FIRE IS THE STATE IN WHICH a situation feels uncomfortable, emotionally heated, intense, and perhaps quite personal. Fire is as pervasive in human interactions as it is in nature—and just as necessary. In this chapter we will learn to recognize different forms of group fire, appreciating both the productive or destructive qualities of high-heat meetings. We'll also examine the ways in which our habits of thinking, emotional hot buttons, and egos make us vulnerable to unwise thoughts and actions when we are standing in the heat of human interaction.

We see fire in the halls of government and in the hallways of our elementary schools. It shows up when the leaders of our churches, synagogues, and mosques gather. We feel the fire at town council meetings and industry conferences. When historic adversaries, diverse ethnic groups, and world leaders come together, we expect and usually get fire. When industry leaders, elected officials, scholars, social activists, and citizens come together to deliberate pressing issues like hunger, climate change, and national security, we witness the fire.

Though it may vary in its form, group fire seems not to discriminate on the basis of race, gender, education, economic class, or culture. In a wonderful documentary film titled *Dalai Lama Renaissance*, forty of the West's most innovative and enlightened thinkers were invited to the home of His Holiness in northern India. The guests included religious scholars, writers, at least two quantum physicists, and a psychiatrist. When they arrived, they were asked by the Dalai Lama to work together to come up with a "solution to some of the world's problems" and to identify "the transitions we must make if we're going to survive." What transpires over the course of several days is a portrait of group fire. The esteemed guests could not agree on a format for their discussions, let alone on any solutions. Bickering, interrupting, showboating, or simply getting lost in wishful thinking, they struggled to collaborate. In the midst of the arguing one participant pleaded, "I'd like to feel a little compassion here." One leaves this film with a simultaneous sense of hopelessness ("If these folks can't get it right, how are the rest of us supposed to learn to work together skillfully?") and relief ("Now I don't feel so bad about all of my lousy meetings").

Conflict and emotional intensity are everywhere, and they are often a source of suffering. But high-heat moments are as natural and as necessary to human progress as they are in nature. We need fire in our families, teams, organizations, and communities as much as our prairies and forests need a cyclical blaze to stay healthy. Nothing interesting or innovative has ever really happened in groups without the heat of passion, disagreement, fear, or confusion. In fact, fire is often the best indicator that people care about the issue with which they are struggling. The absence of heat almost always means apathy, suppression, or nonengagement.

GROUP FIRE CAN BE DESTRUCTIVE

As in nature, fire has both creative and destructive potential in meetings. The destructive aspects of group fire are the more familiar to most of us. Here are some of the less pleasant outcomes of group fires when they are not properly tended:

Suffering. When things heat up, people often become fearful and aggressive. With a single spark, dialogue can degrade into aggressive debate, unreasoned argument, and personal attack. Such interactions often result in winners and losers and can cause emotional pain for those on both sides.

Proliferation. Under the right conditions, a single high-heat conversation gone wrong can escalate and spread throughout an organization or community. For several years my wife and I lived in a condominium managed by a homeowners' association. At an annual meeting of the HOA, one member directed some personal and insulting remarks toward the president. For the following year, interactions within the entire community of neighbors—even those not present at the meeting—felt uncomfortable as people tried to figure out which "side" they were on or how to reconcile the rift. Two years after that meeting, trust had still not been fully restored.

Destruction. In a fire, groups often become overwhelmed and stuck in long-established patterns of defensiveness. Energy and goodwill get used up as people talk past one another. Money is invested and reinvested to "deal with" the consequences of false starts and reactive decisions. People burn out and relationships are destroyed.

GROUP FIRE CAN BE CREATIVE

What is the creative potential of fire in groups? How do emotional intensity, messiness, and disagreement serve us? Why on earth would we want to welcome it into our meetings?

Energy. We've known this lesson since the earliest days of humanity. The more difficult an issue, the more energy we need to tackle it. People bring the heat of their convictions and passions into a room, and this very same heat is often the source of discord. But the dissension is nothing more than an affirmation that people are alive and in pursuit of what matters to them.

Illumination. The fire of group adversity or breakdown is often exactly what people need to see an old problem in a completely new light. Conflict and bewilderment are often the necessary precursors to new ways of viewing the current reality and future possibilities. In the fire, people's gifts and limitations are also illuminated for all to see. In this sense fire is a teacher. In Washington State I worked with a governor-appointed task force made up of police investigators, district attorneys, policymakers, and health care and social service professionals. They came together to formulate statewide guidelines on how to investigate the sexual abuse of children in institutions. At moments during the deliberation, strong disagreements and thinly veiled finger-pointing set off some pretty intense debates. During those very uncomfortable conversations the group discovered that each organizational entity had significantly different, sometimes conflicting priorities when it came to investigating this kind of crime. They realized that each agency, in its own way, often undermined the success of an investigation. It was through this realization that the task force established a breakthrough road map for statewide interagency coordination.

Cleansing. Without the heat behind strong advocacy and direct confrontation, issues can accumulate just under the surface, eventually exploding into a more destructive social dynamic. When people are allowed to fully express their emotions and opinions, and when those are acknowledged, that clearing of the air feels like a fresh start.

Regeneration. In forests and other ecosystems, fires enable seeds to germinate and nutrients to be released into the soil. Likewise, groups who learn to use fire productively see it as an important "nutritional" source of learning and development. In coming through the fires of disagreement and confusion, groups learn some of their most important lessons, and the seeds of innovation are sown.

Transformation. About 3,500 years ago a glassblower figured out how to apply heat to a bucket of silica sand mixed with tree ash in order to transform those simple materials into a beautiful vessel. In the same way, organizations, groups, and individuals can come through the intensity of conflict having created new paradigms, reinvented strategies, restructured organizations, and forged never-before-imagined alliances.

As we sat on his back porch one afternoon, the Abraham Path founder William Ury and I recounted such a transformational meeting. He had been in Bethlehem, in the West Bank, hoping to gain local support for the Abraham Path, a hiking route that extends through and connects Middle Eastern countries that have been at war. The purpose of the Abraham Path is to provide a place of connection for people of all faiths and cultures, inviting them to remember their common origins. Ury described what happened in the meeting.

> *Immediately they started to ask us, "Are you with the CIA? Is this part of a Zionist plot? Why are there no Palestinians on your board?" Then they started making demands. You could feel the distrust in the air. There was so much at stake, and I was concerned that this might be the burial of the Abraham Path project. I'd spent three years of my life, my money, and my credibility to arrive at this moment. I kept thinking to myself, "Let go. Abraham's story is about letting go of control and trusting that a wisdom will emerge." I managed to listen and resisted the urge to defend the project. We stuck with the conversation, letting the Palestinian leaders know that there was no way the Abraham Path would succeed unless it served the needs of their people.*

Though no one who hears this story would have predicted it, today Bethlehem is one of the towns where the Abraham Path has the most support from local leaders! A willingness to stand in the fire with people who initially viewed him as the enemy resulted in a remarkable alliance and an innovative vehicle for peace building and reconciliation in a troubled part of the world.

The Anatomy of Group Fire

For those of us who choose to spend our time in groups that are experiencing both the destructive and creative impacts of group fire, it is useful to have a way of understanding and recognizing the different forms such fire can take.

The most common indications of fire are the visible expressions of fear, anger, aggression, and dissent. They are easy to recognize and can often feel overwhelming. In the very first strategic planning process I ever facilitated, the two company owners, brothers who had grown up on the streets of Brooklyn, stood up simultaneously, leaned across the conference table, and began hurling profanities and waving their cigars at each other. I could see team members retreating to the refreshment table and ducking for cover in their notebooks. I was informed later that this was a normal conversation between the two brothers. One person's firestorm is another's cozy campfire.

A more subtle aspect of group fire is found in groups with a history of disappointment and injury. Members feel they have been burnt in the past. They find it difficult to let go of promises broken, insults never retracted, and contributions never acknowledged. Relationships are often tenuous, and people may feel exhausted and hopeless at the outset of the process. These groups are living out the aftermath of unresolved or poorly handled conflicts and of wounds inflicted during hardfought battles. The groups may appear to have no heat, no motivation. However, more often their members are simply alienated, resigned, and filled with self-protective cynicism. They feel hesitant to offer what little energy they have left. This kind of despair is contagious, and it takes a strong leader to be the sole holder of possibility in a room full of defeat. The inner capacity of *holding possibility* will be explored further in chapter 5.

Another common facet of group fire is the often-silent struggle with uncertainty, doubt, and impatience. Like smoke, uncertainty and complexity create discomfort and obscure people's ability to see clearly. People can feel overwhelmed by the diversity of perspectives, the intricacy of issues, and the sheer number of ideas. Often, in an effort to ease distress and embarrassment, those "in charge," including the process facilitator, will attempt to oversimplify an issue or make a preemptive decision that returns the group to its comfort zone. But this kind of response undermines the group's capacity and perpetuates longstanding problems.

Destructive aspects of group heat have a way of showing up not only in high-stakes meetings but also in what we might have predicted to be routine, noncontroversial conversations. I'm often surprised by the way a casual comment such as "When is the lunch break?" or a subtle behavior like a side conversation can ignite my insecurities or provoke harsh, judgmental thoughts. Collaborative work has a way of inviting into the room all the lessons we need to learn about ourselves.

The Fire Within

Being a competent leader with a history of success has a little-discussed dark side. I've struggled with it most of my career. It is the belief that I can single-handedly hold a group process together and ensure the success of a meeting. I have often assigned too much importance to my role and too adamantly justified my views. I have too often looked to others to affirm my worth and contributions. In some ways, the more successful I have become, the more I find myself needing to acknowledge and gently confront these tendencies.

The rooms in which we work are often places of uneasiness. In the midst of conflict, confusion, and strong emotion, the heat is hard to miss. We hear people raising their voices or using inflammatory language. We watch them taking sides or working unspoken agendas. We see people rolling their eyes with disbelief or withdrawing entirely from the conversation.

As we face these moments of group intensity, we see things that annoy, embarrass, and frighten us. We experience self-doubt and feel overwhelmed. Our own actions or inaction in the moment are part of the fire. Are we making things better, or worse? Is the group beyond help, or are we just not smart enough to know what to do next?

When we get swept up in the group's heat, we want desperately to regain a sense of personal comfort. In order to achieve this, we might try to suppress what we feel, becoming very mechanical in our response. We might attempt to rescue group members, take sides, blame others, or try to control people and outcomes through subtle manipulation. We might argue vehemently or withdraw into passivity. While these responses are normal in the sense that they protect us, they do little to aid the group in achieving its purpose or building its capacity to work through its reactions.

HABITS OF THE MIND

Each of us has unique habits of seeing, thinking, and doing. Our mental habits are the default beliefs about the way things are and the way they ought to be. They form over the course of our lives, based on our experiences, upbringing, education, and so on. They influence our judgments and interpretations. When we take our default way of seeing as the only way to see things, we are what author Ellen Langer calls "engaged in mindlessness."[1] Habits of the mind are particularly dangerous in the fire when we decide what is "acceptable," "appropriate," and "attainable" and don't question our assumptions.

As interactions become more intense, challenging, and personal, our minds fill with interpretations, memories, regrets, predictions, attachments, and resentments. We burn ourselves when we fail to remember that an infinite number of legitimate points of view can be taken on any given topic or situation.

You may see a challenging question from a group member as an insult to your authority, while another sees it as an invitation into dialogue. Still another may see it as a politically motivated move. It all depends on your habitual way of seeing things. The key is to be willing to hold your default beliefs and assumptions up for inspection, never assuming that they are the only truth in the room. We'll examine the specific capacities related to maintaining an open mind in chapter 5.

EMOTIONAL HOT BUTTONS

In the fire, people and events can press up against our hot buttons—those places within us that feel susceptible and, at times, raw. Personal hot buttons grow out of trials and traumas in our lives. Some of us have hot buttons that get triggered by authority, rudeness, crying, or illogic. Others have hot buttons connected to not being liked or approved of by others. Each of us has different hot buttons, and it's important to know what they are.

The people, behavior, and events that push our hot buttons don't need to be dramatic or even visible to others. They can be as subtle as a raised eyebrow or a question about a suggested decision-making method. My hot button in the law enforcement meeting I described in the introduction wasn't the guns, the silence of the group, the divided room, or the palpable hostility. Any of those things could have been hot buttons, but they were not mine on that day. My hot button was the realization that I did not know what to do. At that early stage in my career, my whole professional identity was based on being the one in the room who always knew what to do and didn't have to ask. In my mind, visible uncertainty was a form of failure. I felt ashamed. As a result, my ability to see what was happening in the group, tap in to my wisdom, and take effective action was greatly compromised—not by the group's fire but by my self-inflicted heat. I was unconsciously allowing the group's fire to ignite myself into a state of panic.

When our hot buttons get pushed, the brain mobilizes to defend us from experiencing negative emotions, thoughts, and sensations. Our initial reaction is aimed at protecting ourselves from feeling the underlying trauma. Before our higher intelligence can intervene, it gets commandeered by primitive parts of the brain and we go into fight-or-flight mode. We might become defensive, argumentative, or self-righteous. These impulsive responses—very human default reactions—comfort us, but they can also undermine our ability to take deliberate action in service to the group. What makes hot buttons even more challenging is that the brain appears to be wired to prevent or reverse a fear response once it's triggered.[2]

IDENTITY AND EGO

Research has consistently demonstrated that we humans are prone to see ourselves as more capable, likable, self-aware, and selfless than we actually are.[3] But when we identify too strongly with any quality, we set ourselves up for disappointment.[4] The influence of ego is a reality, particularly when we are working in high-heat situations. I use the term *ego* not in the formal Freudian sense but as shorthand for one's idealized self-image or the stories we tell ourselves and others about who we are.

The people, behavior, and events that push our hot buttons don't need to be dramatic or even visible to others. They can be as subtle as a raised eyebrow or a question about a suggested decision-making method.

The problem comes when reality collides with the inflated self-image we've worked hard to construct. I like to think of myself as someone who is sensitive to the needs of all kinds of people. Recently it was pointed out to me during a workshop that some of the experiential exercises were designed in ways that excluded people with certain kinds of physical disabilities. I worked hard in the moment to correct the oversight, but inside, I was distracted by feelings of shame that in a very public setting, I had not lived up to the image of myself as "enlightened" regarding differences in physical ability. And in that moment, I had to remind myself that my ego was messing with me.

Our ego fuels our need to win, to be right, to be superior. The ego is the part of us that equates our worth with our reputation and achievements. So when something about a meeting begins to go off track, and group confusion or an impasse makes the hoped-for outcomes less likely, we fear we won't live up to our self-image. When we don't know what to do as things become messier, we feel self-conscious and embarrassed about asking for help. We feel psychologically at risk, and this can trigger a kind of fight-or-flight response. In these moments, unless we can acknowledge that the image of ourselves we have constructed is an illusion, we remain in our own fire.

WE BURN OURSELVES

Here's the good news: There is no heat unless we inflict it upon ourselves. Regardless of how hot the fire gets "out there" in the meeting, we have the ability to control our own thermostat. The fire does not determine how intensely we experience the heat. *We* determine that. We determine whether we move into habitual patterns of fighting, fleeing, or freezing in the face of uncomfortable group dynamics. The ability to choose our own internal state in the face of external heat is the essence of intentional, high-integrity leadership. It dictates whether we will be able to offer calm presence and wise action when they are most needed.

We know that the heat is of our own making because two people in the same room at the same high-heat moment can experience that moment in very different ways. The master facilitator and author Roger Schwarz told me about a meeting he co-facilitated early in his career. He was in a union–management meeting when a conflict began to escalate. Participants began raising their voices, making accusations, and threatening to walk out. He recalls the perspiration dripping from his forehead. In his moment of panic, he looked over at his co-facilitator, who was older and more experienced. His colleague, smiling from ear to ear, said, "Wow, this is really getting interesting, isn't it?"

That is a hopeful story. We think we are navigating a big group storm, and then we realize we have manufactured the storm. The consultant Chris Corrigan described his insight that fires and storms are really illusions. Chris said, "Difficult situations are made difficult by me to a much larger extent than by others. It's really a storm depending on how I see it. . . . When I am fearless, I am just standing in a rain shower."[5] As we will see in the next chapter, doing our own work on our fears enables us to control our personal thermostats when we face the heat out there. We can learn to see, hear, and sense the intense heat in groups without taking it on ourselves. We don't need to be impervious or above it all. Nor do we need to avoid having our hot buttons pushed. Our buttons will get pushed. Our personal vulnerabilities will appear as they show up in the group's dynamic, like a mirror into our psyche. But we don't have to act on them. Nor do we need to suppress them. As we'll explore in chapter 11, we can develop practices that aid us in noticing strong emotional reactions without allowing them to take over. We can learn to experience the pull of strong feelings without abandoning our inner wisdom and good judgment.

Our work throughout the rest of this book is to let the fire we create within ourselves become the teacher that strengthens our capacity to stand purposefully when a calm, compassionate, unwavering leader is most needed. Our hot-button moments are really moments of truth that point to the places where we need to open our hearts and minds rather than collapse into self-protection. These moments when we can feel the fire within are, as the Buddhist teacher Pema Chödrön says, "like messengers that show us, with terrifying clarity, exactly where we're stuck."[6] Our self-generated fire is a messenger that carries insights into what it means to lead with clarity, calm, and courage. It is through these deeply personal, sometimes painful insights that we learn to stand in the intensity of group fire and tend its creative potential.

WHEN PEOPLE COME TOGETHER TO ADDRESS HIGH-stakes issues, things can get heated—emotionally intense, uncomfortable, and at times personal. This is group fire. It's pervasive, natural, and necessary to human progress. Without the heat of passion and conviction, meetings rarely produce anything interesting or innovative. Because group fire can also be a source of destruction and suffering, we need to learn to channel its energy. Tending to the heat without being swept up by it is the challenge of standing well in the fire.

QUESTIONS FOR REFLECTION

▣ Think about the last high-heat meeting you facilitated. What were the indicators that the group was experiencing high heat? What did people say and do?

▣ Did a recent event or individual in a meeting push one of your hot buttons? What was your response in the moment? What did you feel? What were you thinking to yourself?

▣ When you are leading groups, what causes you to feel defensive, impatient, or anxious? What internal narratives and beliefs are connected with these feelings?

▣ What are the unrealistic or perfectionist expectations you have of yourself as a meeting convener? In what situations do you begin to feel stressed or vulnerable because you are not living up to those expectations?

- Have you experienced a time when you felt like reacting but you were able to make a more intentional choice rather than react from impulsiveness or defensiveness? What enabled you to do this?

TRY THIS

As you go about your daily and weekly activities, notice which interactions have heat and what form it takes. Where are you noticing high levels of passion and conviction? Where do things appear to be contentious or personal? When do you notice the absence of fire in group interactions? Notice your judgments and emotions as you observe and participate in the heat of daily interactions. Take a moment to write down what you would most like to learn about group fire and about yourself as someone who convenes people in high-heat conversations.

WE ARE
FIRE TENDERS

I get paid for two things. First is my ability in

difficult and scary moments to pay attention to

spoken and unspoken dimensions. Second is my

willingness to feel overwhelmed and confused,

and move into that rather than to sidestep it.

—Saul Eisen, PhD

Developing Human Systems

IT'S NOT ENOUGH TO BE A knowledgeable and insightful leader with adequate meeting-management skills. We must become masterful conveners. Among the most challenging aspects of convening —bringing diverse people together to achieve a common purpose—are the struggles and tensions that will inevitably arise.

In any collaborative effort, people bring widely different and often conflicting points of view to the table. To make things more challenging, they usually feel very attached to their points of view. They also come to the conversation with different levels of hope and doubt, a range of interpersonal skills, and varied agendas. As described in the previous chapter, discomfort, frustration, and confusion are bound to show up as people make honest efforts to find common ground amid their differences. They need people in the room who can shine the light of calm presence and clear purpose when others are escalating or shutting down in the heat of a challenging moment.

We must become fire tenders—people who can stand in the face of incendiary conflicts and perplexing challenges and help others hold the tensions, emotions, and uncertainties long enough to arrive at new insights and common ground. This chapter describes the role of leaders as fire tenders and how our *way of being* in high-heat conversations represents a frontier for breakthrough leadership.

And Now, a Message from the U.S. National Forest Service

A common misconception is that we need to keep the peace in our institutions by suppressing anything that is controversial, loud, emotional, or potentially polarizing. Anything that might spark a conflict is discouraged. But attempts to prevent or suppress uncertainty, conflict, and emotion produce what fire experts call a "fuel buildup"—a condition that contributes to large, highly destructive fires.

For most of the twentieth century, federal fire policy in the United States focused on suppressing fires in all national forests. This policy, aimed at protecting timber resources and rural communities, ignored the ecological importance of fire. As a result, many of the nation's forests became choked with vegetation, and the accumulated grass, shrubs, and saplings formed a fuel ladder that enabled fires to climb quickly into forest canopies. The United States began to see a series of conflagrations that destroyed more resources than ever before. Today, the Forest

Service has acknowledged that the indiscriminate policy of suppressing all forest fires was a mistake.

Sadly, many institutions seem to have maintained the Forest Service's policy with the same results. Organizations and communities have a buildup of underbrush—voices not heard, issues not addressed, and "undiscussibles" that need desperately to be discussed. We are beginning to see the conflagrations that have been born out of our suppressive policies: an unprecedented failure of the global financial system, epidemic increases in childhood obesity and diabetes, the disappearance of freshwater, and what the World Wildlife Fund calls the "worst spate of species extinction since the dinosaurs."[1] It's time to let the sparks fly—to unleash the voices of concern, to express the unpopular truths, and to examine every inch of the proverbial elephant in the room.

To do this, we need to become fire tenders. Fire tending doesn't mean unleashing an unbridled wildfire. Nor does it imply that we will become the sole caretaker or rescuer of those involved in high-heat deliberations. It means assisting people in facing intensely heated conflicts and perplexing challenges, holding the tensions, emotions, and uncertainties long enough to arrive at new insights, common ground, and a commitment to action.

A Tale of Two Bus Drivers

As fire tenders, the most powerful tool we have is our presence. Our mindset, emotional state, and the way we occupy physical space have a profound impact on those around us.

I see an example of this influence every time I commute to and from the local airport via the public bus system. Going to the airport I frequently have the same bus driver, whom we can refer to as George. From the moment I encounter George, I sense that I am an inconvenience to him. It's not that George is rude. He loads my luggage, takes the fare, announces the various stops, and gets me safely to the airport. But somehow I sense anger just under the surface of George's demeanor. I can feel it in my body during the entire one-hour journey between Boulder and the Denver airport. If I am not conscious about what is happening, I leave the bus carrying not only my luggage but also the emotional baggage of George's anger.

On the return bus trip back home, a man we'll call Fred is often my driver. Like George, Fred is a man of few words. He performs the same responsibilities as George. Fred greets me, loads luggage, takes fares, announces the stops, and gets me home from the airport safely and on time. But there is a powerful difference. My initial encounters with Fred feel welcoming and warm, and I feel cared for, safe, and generally optimistic.

These two men have the same job, follow the same procedures, communicate with similar words, and drive the identical routes, but the difference in their presence is indisputable. We have all had this kind of experience. We walk into a room of people and sense joy, optimism, tension, or despair almost immediately. Like George and Fred, each of us is a kind of conductor, not in the sense of driving a bus, but as a transmitter of energy.

The Illusion of Our Separateness

Though much has been written on the need for facilitators and mediators to maintain a "professional distance"—standing separate and apart from others—there is growing evidence that we are in a constant and invisible but profoundly felt transaction with one another. We "touch" others without making physical contact. Recent social neuroscience research supports the idea that the way we show up with each other matters. According to the internationally known psychologist Daniel

Goleman, mirror neurons are a kind of "emotional Wi-Fi" that keeps us tuned in to what is happening in other people. This system tracks movements, emotions, and intentions, and it activates in our brains the precise areas that are active in the other person's brain. Essentially, we are instantaneously and unconsciously put on the same emotional wavelength as the people in our field of consciousness. Our emotions and moods are infectious.[2]

Neuroscience also states strongly that the internal state of the leader affects the internal state of others, that those viewed as having authority have the power to cast light or darkness onto a meeting. Goleman asserts that the social intelligence that enables one to be aware of this dynamic is the lifeblood of an excellent leader. He writes, "Leaders have to take more responsibility for their impact on the people they lead and the people around them. And every co-worker does as well."[3] Given the insight that we literally shape each other's brains, it's no wonder that my airport commutes with George and Fred feel like night and day. While I have a choice in the matter of how I feel during these commutes, the invisible transaction of emotions is unquestionably a very real part of the journey.

While a stance of impartiality is often essential to the role we play in a deliberation, the group always affects us, just as we affect the group. Separateness is an illusion. As we make our best attempts at neutrality, we are undeniably part of the system. Fire tenders must learn to be aware of and embrace these moment-to-moment influences even as we strive for impartiality.

Being a Masterful Fire Tender

Masterful fire tenders have an uncanny ability to stand in the face of high-heat interactions and not get knocked off balance, even as others around them do. They maintain their calm, clarity, curiosity, and resoluteness, even as others become adversarial, confused, or resigned to "another failed attempt to resolve this issue."

The journey of mastery for fire tenders involves three dimensions. First, we must acquire *knowledge*. We must have a working paradigm that provides a lens for understanding individual, group, and larger system dynamics. We must also develop an understanding of the systems in which the group members work, the issues they face, and the questions with which they seek to wrestle.

Second, fire tenders must develop *skills* in a wide variety of facilitative techniques. We become skillful through practice, self-reflection, and feedback. Over time, we develop our own personal inventory of nuanced tools that serve us well in a wide variety of situations.

Too often, training in facilitative leadership stops there. We think that knowing *what* and *how* are enough. But as Marianne Hughes, a thirty-year veteran of high-heat meetings, says, knowledge and skills are not sufficient: "We have a methodology and extraordinarily skilled and well-trained consultants, but that would never be enough to do the work."[4] What is often neglected is the third critical dimension of mastery for fire tenders. It is the dimension of *who* we are being as we use our considerable knowledge and skills. It is what accounts for the difference between the two bus drivers. This dimension deals with the presence we bring to our work—our mental, emotional, and physical state.

Through self-awareness and conscious choices we become the authors of our leadership contribution rather than allowing the fire to trigger us into defensive, unwitting responses. We can face the heat while still accessing our inner resources—our accumulated knowledge and skills. Masterful fire tenders have many ways to stand effectively in the fire:

- As the fire forces them to face their own self-limiting ways of thinking, emotional hot buttons, and ego, they stand with deep self-awareness.

- When others become mired in remembrances of past failures and predictions of impending disaster, they stand in the present, grounded in the here and now.

- Adroit fire tenders will not allow judgments and biases to cloud what they see and choose to do from moment to moment. This is the stance of receptivity, or "open-mindedness."

- In the face of confusion and uncertainty, masterful fire tenders remain in service to the group's purpose, standing with clarity about what they must stand for in the moment.

- As surprises and disruptions occur, great fire tenders respond with the fluidity, spontaneity, and grace of a dancer.

- When individual or group dynamics become distasteful or uncomfortable to witness, consummate fire tenders find a way to sustain compassion, standing with a wide-open heart.

Fire tending is not a job description as much as it is a set of capacities that can be cultivated. Fire tenders recognize that skills are important, but they also know that their presence is the essential instrument for change. They commit to a lifelong journey of self-understanding and personal practice. They don't aspire to a state of perfection. Their goal is simply to bring their full, most conscious, and deliberate self to each interaction in order to serve as an instrument for positive change.

Fire tenders see every day as an opportunity to practice stepping toward the things that they would much rather steer clear of—toward the certainty of uncertainty, the possibility of failure, and the likelihood of painful self-realization.

The gift of fire tending is that each time we bring the fullness of ourselves to the work of positive change, we are ourselves changed. Each time that we can be what Edwin Friedman calls "the non-anxious presence"[5] in groups, institutions, and communities where anxiety is pervasive, we come to trust our being over motivational or manipulative techniques. Each time that we tend to groups in which people transform their confusion, suffering, and resignation into hope, healing, and responsibility, we feel greater confidence that who we are as we lead really does matter.

Why Does Our Interior State of Being Matter?

Fire tenders recognize that standing well in the face of high-heat situations means cultivating a special state of mental, emotional, physical, and spiritual being. Some may wonder, *Can't I be an instrument of positive change without having to worry about my inner state?* The answer is no.

Our interior state affects many aspects of our performance and a group's dynamic. Our inner state influences how we see and interpret reality. Our moods, emotions, and assumptions form a powerful lens that colors our perception. Our inner state also affects what options we perceive to be available in any given moment. If we are feeling cynicism or self-doubt, we may see different and perhaps fewer ways in which we might be of service to a group that is struggling. Additionally, in these emotional states, we might not be as agile in choosing an appropriate or productive course of action.

If as leaders we regularly get caught up in the fire of competition, confusion, and fear, succumbing to our more defensive and reactive nature, we enable those dysfunctional patterns to perpetuate themselves in our teams, organizations, and communities. Alternatively, a centered interior state can set the stage for new social patterns in which people learn to hold uncomfortable tensions, uncertainties, and emotions while they work creatively to find solutions. The spiritual teacher Marianne Williamson captured the essence of this idea when she wrote, "As we let our own light shine, we unconsciously give other people permission to do the same. As we are liberated from our own fear, our presence automatically liberates others."[6] The work of fire tenders is to cultivate and offer this kind of liberating presence.

It's Hard Work; It's the Most Important Work

Over the long term, nobody remembers what you said or did. They rarely remember the specific decisions made in meetings. Instead, they remember how they felt in your presence and in the presence of one another. And how that feeling somehow enabled them to become more—more creative, more open, and more resolute in solving a really tough problem.

We fire tenders often stand in the intensity of scorching conversations when voices are raised, arms flail, and people get increasingly uncomfortable. In such moments, our job is to aid the group in directing the heat of its passion, fear, and confusion toward a productive purpose.

To accomplish this, we must divest ourselves of our long-ingrained beliefs about what it means to be a "real leader"—someone who has the answers, takes charge when things get uncomfortable, stands in complete objectivity, and shows no emotion. Shedding our survival impulses and rejecting the external pressures to be the great rescuer is the fire tender's work of a lifetime.

We can't access or effectively share our skills, knowledge, and accumulated wisdom with others unless we come to understand the secret to being a masterful fire tender. *The path to becoming a truly effective instrument of change is in the conscious tending of our own fires—attending to what is going on inside us in order to clearly see and intentionally assist in the unfolding of what is happening outside us.*

Attending to our own fires is our most important work. To live and lead with purpose means that in our efforts to influence people and events we will inevitably confront the unpredictable consequences of who we are being while we are leading. It means coming face-to-face with the reality of who we are in contrast to the self-image we have spent a lifetime constructing.

Whether our purposeful contribution to the world takes the form of leadership, facilitation, mediation, teaching, coaching, or social activism, we can all cultivate the capacity to be a fire tender in the face of human firestorms. We need only believe that the work of changing the world begins with cultivating our own human potential.

FIRE TENDERS STAND IN THE FACE OF INCENDIARY conflicts and perplexing challenges, helping others stick with uncertainty, troubling emotions, and conflict long enough to arrive at new insights and common ground. This kind of leadership involves learning to face those things we most fear—to sit in the midst of intense personal discomfort, to resist acting on old stories and impulses, and to be present to what is emerging in the group and within ourselves. The path to becoming a masterful fire tender is in the conscious tending of our own fires—attending to what is going on inside us in order to assist in the unfolding of what is happening outside us. Pursuing this path requires that we learn to *stand* in new ways.

▩ What conversations have been suppressed in your family, organization, or community? When have you been guilty of suppressing a difficult conversation in the name of keeping the peace or keeping things on track?

▩ What qualities of fire tender do you see in the leaders you most admire? What qualities of fire tender do you see in yourself?

▩ When you think about yourself as an instrument of positive change, how does your mental, emotional, and physical presence—your way of being—come into play?

▩ Can you recall a time when your beliefs, assumptions, or emotions got in the way of working effectively in a high-heat situation? What did you learn about yourself?

TRY THIS

Pick someone who has formal or informal authority in a group to which you belong. Over the course of several meetings, observe this person's emotional state and any positive or negative impacts this seems to have on the group members, including you.

Next, pay attention to your emotional state when you lead meetings. Check your physical energy, feelings, and mood as you begin. How would you describe your feelings? Do you choose to make any adjustments prior to the meeting? What do you notice to be the relationship between your inner state and energy during the meeting and what you observe in others?

SIX WAYS
OF STANDING

Now that we have examined the nature of fire and the role we play as fire tenders, let's look at the ways we can stand effectively in the face of high-heat group dynamics. Standing is really a metaphor for *being*. When we are working with groups that are struggling with adversity, complexity, and the intense emotions of the moment, *who we are being*—the nature of our presence in the room—is as powerful an intervention as anything we do or say. Even the most basic facilitation intervention, such as asking a clarifying question, has a fundamentally different impact on a group when it is asked from a stance of relaxed openness and compassion versus a stance of defensiveness or anxiety.

This section describes six ways of standing (see the figure on the next page). We could think about and work on each of these stances as if they were separate and distinct. But they are not. They are interconnected, overlapping, and mutually supportive. They also occur simultaneously. In any given moment we rarely manifest only one way of standing. More likely, especially when things get tense, we draw on multiple stances all at once to stay centered

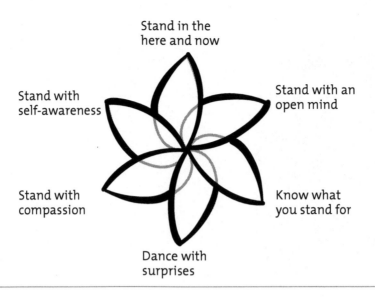

Stand in the
here and now

Stand with an
open mind

Stand with
self-awareness

Know what
you stand for

Stand with
compassion

Dance with
surprises

and in service to the group. It's useful to think about these six ways of standing as a flowing, dynamic dance rather than a static pose. To stand in the fire, you must learn to:

- Stand with self-awareness
- Stand in the here and now
- Stand with an open mind
- Know what you stand for
- Dance with surprises
- Stand with compassion

For each of these ways of standing we will look first at how we burn ourselves—in other words, at what can go wrong when we are not conscious and deliberate in choosing how we stand. Then we'll explore what it means to stand in each way, what capacities we need to master that way of standing, and what aspects of our work shift when we learn to stand in that way.

Teaching ourselves to stand well—to adopt a productive mental, emotional, and physical state of being—yields tangible payoffs for us and for the people in our meetings:

- We avoid falling back on a few "old reliable" ways of responding and can see a broader array of choices in any given moment.

- We avoid getting clouded by emotion and confusion and can readily access our accumulated knowledge and innate wisdom.
- We consistently act with the purpose of serving others rather than ourselves.
- We see, hear, and feel what is happening in the group and within ourselves with greater clarity.
- We recover more quickly after an emotional hot button is pushed.
- We are less susceptible to stress and fatigue.
- We are able to act with greater flexibility, courage, and integrity instead of getting swept up in the moment.

I offer these six ways of standing to help you understand and shape your interior experience as you lead. Ultimately, I hope that as you internalize these mindsets and develop the capacities associated with each way of standing, the six categories will become less important and you will find the flow of your own unique dance.

■

STAND WITH SELF-AWARENESS

The existence of limiting beliefs and thoughts is good news. It means that reality, as we experience it when we are stressed or angry or stuck, is more malleable than it often feels.

—Caitlin M. Frost

Facilitator and Coach,

Harvest Moon Consultants

AS FIRE TENDERS, HOW DO WE AVOID being swept away in the heat of a group? More accurately, how do we minimize the heat we create for ourselves when interactions in the group become intense or personal? This chapter is based on a simple premise: Self-awareness is the foundation for wise action. The better observers we become of our mental, emotional, and physical states, the more mindful our responses will be when we are standing in the fire. In other words, the more intimately we can come to know our emotional hot buttons, the better we are able to act from choice rather than impulse. The more we recognize our habitual and ego-driven ways of thinking, the more likely we are to speak and act in ways that serve the group.

How Do We Burn Ourselves?

Each of us experiences two worlds. The first is the world of external reality—the things, people, and events happening out there. The second is the world within our heads—the interior realm of thoughts, feelings, impulses, insecurities, attractions, and aversions. We navigate between both of these worlds each day, making fluid transitions and hardly noticing that they are distinct realms. We get into trouble when we forget that our thoughts and emotions are distinct from the world out there. The less aware we are of our interior world, the more susceptible we are to being confined or swept away by our self-created stories and feelings about what's happening out there.

Emotions are an asset without which humans could not have survived through the ages. In the face of danger, emotions produce changes in the brain and autonomic nervous system that mobilize us into doing what's necessary to deal with the danger. All this takes place in a split second without our having to consciously think about what's happening.

According to the researcher Paul Eckman, humans have "auto-appraisers," mechanisms that enable us to unconsciously and continuously scan our environment for events that we learn to associate with different emotions—fear, sadness, surprise, joy, anger, and so on. Over the course of our lives, the mind creates an "emotional alert database" that contains an ever-expanding list of shortcut themes that guide the auto-appraiser. These themes have great potency for eliciting an emotional reaction, especially the themes established in early childhood experiences.[1] We can call these hot buttons or triggers. For example, I was bullied as a child at school, and I have learned over the years that one of my hot buttons is pushed when people try to impose their authority over me. If my auto-appraiser senses even the slightest hint that I might be backed against the wall (in either physical or psychological terms) by someone with more power, I am prone to react with fear and aggression. I've had to learn over the course of adulthood that this response serves neither me nor the group.

HOW THOUGHTS AND EMOTIONS CAN GET US INTO TROUBLE

Our ability to scan the environment and instantaneously mobilize emotional and neurological responses works wonderfully if we need to escape from a saber-toothed tiger or an oncoming bus. But as Eckman points out, our emotions can get us into trouble in three ways.[2] First, we may feel and show the appropriate emotion but at a magnitude disproportionate to what the situation calls for. For example, we may have reason to feel frustrated with a group that is becoming side-tracked, but if our frustration escalates into anger, it is counterproductive.

Second, we may feel an appropriate emotion but then demonstrate it the wrong way. For example, anxiety about how little time remains in the meeting may be justified, but if we express that anxiety by cutting people off in midsentence, it's not so useful.

Third, we might feel an altogether inappropriate emotion, based on a sensitive hot button or an erroneous perception. In this case, the problem isn't that we become too angry or show anxiety in the wrong way. It is that there is no real cause to become angry or anxious. We simply got triggered when we didn't need to be.

I let myself be needlessly triggered in this way many years ago when I worked with Elizabeth Glazer, who in the face of her own battle with AIDS cofounded the Pediatric AIDS Foundation. When I arrived for a meeting with the three other cofounders, I was told that the time and location of the meeting had been changed. I immediately felt resentful that they had waited until the last minute to inform me. I told myself, "They are being inconsiderate, and they don't appreciate the value of the pro bono services I'm offering." Apparently my facial expression conveyed this without my saying a word, because one of the cofounders leaned over and whispered in my ear, "Elizabeth's health has deteriorated, and we need to move the meeting to her bedside at home." That's the day I learned that I had a hot button related to not being appreciated.

Once we're in a strong emotional state, we look for information aimed at confirming, justifying, or maintaining that emotion. For example, we may feel ashamed after being publicly criticized. Even if some people are also saying that we are doing a great job, we have difficulty integrating the positive information. In these moments, we feel absolutely certain that our negative interpretations are correct and complete. This is what psychologists call the *refractory state*. According to Eckman, the refractory state is a period in which our thinking "cannot incorporate information that does not fit, maintain, or justify the emotion we are feeling."[3] If this state lasts for more than a few seconds, it distorts the way we perceive the world and ourselves.

THE CONSEQUENCES OF BEING EMOTIONALLY TRIGGERED

Getting emotionally triggered undermines our ability to hold the gathering space with integrity. Here are the most common consequences of hot-button moments:

- When we get stuck in a particular emotion, we are less able to access our personal resources—our knowledge, skills, and creativity that would otherwise be available if we weren't in a triggered state.

- When gripped by a strong emotion, our seeing becomes very biased. We interpret what is happening in a way that fits with how we are feeling, and at the same time, we tend to ignore any knowledge that doesn't fit with our emotional state.

- In the midst of a strong emotional reaction, our primary preoccupation is restoring our own comfort. In this state it's difficult to extend understanding and compassion to others.

- Even after we realize we have misperceived a situation and need not be emotional, the emotion often persists. The momentum of a strong emotion can pull us away from impartiality and into further story making.

The purpose of self-awareness is not to repress our emotions when we get triggered. Through self-awareness we recognize our limiting internal narratives and feelings as normal but not always useful parts of ourselves, and in that moment of recognition we can create space for choice to occur. That space allows us to examine our interpretations and reactions, breathe deeply, and consider alternative responses that have more integrity for us and that support the purpose of the meeting.

What Does It Mean to Stand with Self-Awareness?

Imagine yourself standing in front of a full-length mirror, taking stock of what you see. There are now two versions of the self. One self is observing, and the other self is observed. The sole purpose of the observer is to study the other with the goal of understanding his or her patterns and motives and becoming self-aware.

Without self-awareness we live in a world where everything we see, think, and feel becomes the indisputable truth. Without self-awareness every choice is self-righteous, and every action self-justified. For some, walking through the world without self-awareness can be a form of ignorant bliss. But for leaders, it is a debilitating form of blindness that causes suffering for them and for those with whom they work.

Every time a hot button is pushed, every time we notice ourselves feeling stuck, resistant to new feedback, harshly judgmental, or physically uncomfortable, it is an invitation to stand in front of the mirror. I was once facilitating a board meeting of a manufacturers' association. The board was deliberating on whether to keep its long-established trade show in New York or move it to a more affordable and centrally located city. About halfway through the meeting, the doors of the conference room swung open and in walked the mayor of New York, accompanied by a fifteen-person entourage of bodyguards and economic development staff members. This was a complete surprise to everyone in the room, especially me. I was asked to sit down while the mayor made a twenty-minute plea to the group to keep the trade show in New York. In that moment I felt intimidated and deferent, and I literally could not speak. I remained seated and silent until I was advised to carry on facilitating the meeting. No other city's mayor had an opportunity to address the board before a decision was made, and I've always felt that this skewed the decision in a way that made the process unfair.

When I look back on that moment, I see how my own pattern of deference to fame and status may have undermined my ability to act in service to my client's higher purpose and to my own values about creating "fair playing fields." With more self-awareness I might have recognized myself shrinking back, named what was happening, and quickly huddled with the meeting chair to discuss the implications of the mayor's unanticipated presentation. The time I've taken to reflect on this pattern has provided me with the ability to more quickly recognize it when it begins to manifest itself. The "defer to fame and status" hot button still exists, but my awareness of it has made it less powerful.

What Capacities Must We Cultivate to Stand with Self-Awareness?

Each moment in the fire is a teacher if we stand in front of the mirror. How do we stay alert to our mental, emotional, and physical states during high-heat moments? The capacities that enable us to maintain a high level of moment-to-moment self-awareness while standing in the fire are *self-observation*, *whole-body sensing*, and *reflective processing*.

SELF-OBSERVATION

What have you learned to notice over the course of your career working with groups? Chances are, you can recite many dimensions of group dynamics. It's likely you are well versed in what to watch and listen for in group member behavior. But how about you? To what extent do you examine the ebbs and flows of your own thoughts and feelings?

The capacity of self-observation involves stepping back and systematically watching ourselves as carefully as we watch the group. Self-observation involves asking ourselves a basic question: *What's up with me?* The purpose of the question is to name thoughts and feelings that may be percolating only at the periphery of our consciousness but are having an impact on how we show up in our work. As we ask this question, we can look at a number of dimensions of the self.

Conscious thoughts. These are thoughts of which we are fully or partially aware. In observing conscious thoughts, it's particularly helpful to identify the *limiting beliefs* and stories we carry with us. The consultant and thought leader Peter Block describes such beliefs as inducing "fear, separation, and blame."[4] Examples include:

I know best.

My job is to control this meeting.

They're to blame for this mess.

If they don't achieve the meeting goal, it's my failure.

He should not be so emotional.

These kinds of thoughts make up our inner dialogue and form a significant portion of the lens through which we see ourselves and the world. Naming them through self-observation is a critical first step toward examining their impact and making more conscious choices.

Unconscious thoughts. We have secrets we keep even from ourselves. One dimension of the unconscious that has a particularly high impact on leaders is what Carl Jung called the *shadow*. Shadow beliefs relate to repressed, disowned, or unresolved weaknesses, shortcomings, and drives we all carry with us. Examples of shadow beliefs include *I am not good enough* or *I need to be right all the time*. One way to observe the shadow is to notice things we are not willing to say in the first person (*I am afraid*). Instead we push it away or project it onto the second person (*I am not afraid, but you sure are*) or the third person (*The world is a scary place*). Putting words to our shadows is an important aspect of self-awareness and the first step toward transforming them.

Emotions and hot buttons. The purpose of observing our emotional patterns is to "map" our hot buttons. As we learn the landscape of our emotions, we become more able to anticipate when we might be pulled into a reactive response. As we learn to observe and name our emotions in the moment, we also put ourselves in a more advantageous position to diffuse or redirect the particular emotional energy that has grabbed us. The Try This exercise at the conclusion of this chapter is a useful practice for identifying your hot buttons.

Moods. While emotions tend to come and go in minutes or seconds, moods are more enduring and tend to be milder than emotions. Someone in a gloomy mood might be slightly sad nearly all the time. Someone in a hostile mood might be slightly angry for long periods. Negative moods distort our thinking. They make it more difficult for us to control what we do. Being able to identify that a mood is at play is the essential first step toward minimizing any negative impact of the mood on our work.

Attractions and aversions. Humans want to maximize those things that give them pleasure and minimize those things that cause discomfort or pain in either a psychological or a physical sense. Our attractions and aversions are working on us all the time. They color how we see things and what we are feeling. For example, over the years I have learned that I take great pleasure in the accolades I receive from meeting participants. I also know that I have to be careful that this praise does not seduce me into making poor facilitation choices. Likewise, I have to be careful that when things are not going well and there are no compliments to be found, I don't become distracted or resentful. The more able we are to name our sources of attraction and aversion, the less vulnerable we are to being burnt by them.

Self-observation requires that we learn to distance ourselves from our thoughts and emotions—taking a few steps back from the mirror so that we might have a clearer, more complete view of what's happening. While we can never achieve complete detachment and objectivity regarding our own thoughts and emotions, there is great value in cultivating the capacity of self-observation.

As we become skilled observers of ourselves and learn to name counterproductive thoughts and emotions, we must do so with gentleness. We want to avoid the aggressive pattern of "name and blame" and instead apply a degree of compassion to the process of observing ourselves. Specific capacities related to compassion for the self are explored further in chapter 8.

WHOLE-BODY SENSING

When we get triggered, the reaction shows up first in our bodies. For this reason, physical sensations can carry important information. Specific emotions generate particular patterns of sensation in our bodies. These somatic reactions are noticeable before the emotion is.

While self-observation is a more cognitively based capacity, whole-body sensing is experiential. Over the years, I have come to recognize my "early warning signals" as indicators that an emotional hot button has been pushed. As we come to know our bodies, we learn to associate certain sensations with particular emotions. For example, I have come to recognize that my jaw muscles tighten when I am feeling anger or resentment. I have learned that my speech speeds up when I am feeling stressed or impatient. My face becomes flushed and hot when I am feeling embarrassed or ashamed. This kind of awareness provides me with an opportunity to "see" what is happening early enough so that I can choose what I want to do with the emotion.

Your body can be an ally and teacher. It holds its own wisdom waiting to be unlocked. In *The Anatomy of Change*, Richard Strozzi Heckler wrote, "Working through the body is unearthing a wisdom that is often neglected and denied in our society. This is the wisdom of feeling, compassion, and intuition."[5] We need only become more curious about our physical sensations—to inquire regularly and intentionally into what we are feeling. As we develop the capacity to notice what is happening with our physical sensations, we learn to recognize when we have been or are about to be knocked off balance. We can learn to monitor our breathing pattern, heart rate, body temperature, muscle tension, and many other sensations. Specific practices for whole-body sensing are covered throughout part III.

REFLECTIVE PROCESSING

Recently, I saw a bumper sticker that read, "Don't believe everything your mind tells you." Our perceptions and inferences are often inaccurate—especially when we are experiencing an uncomfortable event or an intense emotion. Reflective processing involves holding our beliefs and assumptions up to the light and examining them by asking questions like, *Is this the only way to look at things?* and, *What does this belief or emotion bring into my life?* Holding our way of seeing as only one among many points of view is an essential quality of the self-aware fire tender. This quality is strengthened through reflective processing.

We need a way to inspect our thoughts for their validity and usefulness in the moment. Writers like Byron Katie and Marilee Adams have developed very useful processes that support reflective processing. At the heart of these practices is self-inquiry—asking ourselves questions aimed at inspecting the truth and utility of the limiting stories we tell ourselves. Self-inquiry practice is examined as an "everyday readiness" practice in chapter 9.

Reflective processing helps us to check the accuracy of our limiting perceptions and interpretations and to explore alternative ways of seeing any given situation. Whenever I am feeling very sure of my viewpoint, I try to picture one of the really smart people I know and ask myself, "How would Hal see this situation right now if he saw it differently than I do?" Here are additional reflective questions that help us examine our inferences and perceptions:

■ What belief or perspective (about others, myself, the situation) do I feel attached to right now?

- Is this belief supported by the facts?

- Do the facts also support alternative ways of seeing this?

- What are the implications of this being true? What will it mean to me if this is not true?

- What is my motivation for being right about this?

- In what way does this belief strengthen or undermine my ability to show up at my best right now?

- In what ways does this belief enable me to help the group achieve its purpose?

In addition to questioning our inferences and perceptions, we can use reflective processing to challenge the appropriateness of an emotion, the intensity of that emotion, and the way the emotion is being expressed. Some reflective questions that enable us to heighten our awareness when we are triggered include:

- What just precipitated this emotion in me?

- What is the story I am telling myself to justify or maintain this emotion?

- Am I meeting the group's needs or my own in this moment?

- If being in this emotional state isn't in service to the group, what is keeping me from doing something about it?

- When I am in this emotional state, which of my gifts do I deny the group?

Our ability to name certain thoughts and feelings for what they are, to recognize bodily sensations as early clues to what might be going on, and to inspect the "stories" we make up in our heads is a valuable capacity that enables us to stand with self-awareness.

What Shifts When We Stand with Self-Awareness?

Learning to stand with self-awareness lays the foundation for the other five ways of standing in the fire. As we become more knowledgeable about our mental and emotional wiring, we bring new sources of positive influence into our work as leaders. Our *connection* with ourselves and others is strengthened, our *resourcefulness* is increased, and we can maintain our *neutrality* more easily.

CONNECTION

Self-awareness acquaints us with many facets of ourselves and teaches us to be more compassionate with our shadow side. As we become more astute about our limiting beliefs and how we get emotionally triggered, we come to feel more empathy for others as they struggle with similar limiting beliefs and emotions. As self-awareness grows, we come to the realization that we are all struggling with what it means to be human, and from that realization springs a greater sense of compassion for and connection with others. As our awareness becomes more finely tuned, we also increase our capacity to tune in to the individual and collective states of others, extending the same compassion and gentleness to them as we do to ourselves.

RESOURCEFULNESS

As conveners of high-heat meetings, we need to make wise choices in service to the groups we are leading. When we are living in the illusion that our beliefs and stories are true, we are living in a world with fewer possibilities. When emotions like fear, anger, and desperation become the pervading lens through which we see a situation, we see only what supports those emotions. In this low state of self-awareness we are like an artist who paints with only one color. Because self-awareness removes the mental and emotional obstructions to our seeing, it enhances our ability to access the fullness of our wisdom and creativity. Self-awareness gives us an expanded range of colors—possibilities and choices—from which to draw.

NEUTRALITY

There will be moments in the fire when people need to trust our impartiality. When we can bring impartiality into the room, others can relax and feel more confident that diverse perspectives will be welcomed. But when we are grabbed by strong emotion, limiting beliefs, or ego, we lose our neutrality. The moment one of these vulnerabilities overcomes us, we tend to focus our attention on restoring our own comfort or validating our view of the world. Although we can never achieve complete objectivity, standing in front of the mirror represents our commitment to continuously monitor whether our mental, emotional, or physical state is in any way obscuring our vision.

STANDING WITH SELF-AWARENESS MEANS ENGAGING a moment-to-moment alertness to the ways that our ego, habitual thought patterns, and emotional hot buttons conspire to pull us into the downward spiral of a group in distress. The better observers we become of our mental, emotional, and physical states, the more mindful our responses from one moment to the next. From the stance of self-awareness we can name our interpretations and feelings without acting on them. Self-awareness moves us toward a decision on which all of the other ways of stand-ing depend: *Do I follow the energy of self-protection and fight-or-flight, or do I create the energy of deliberate action?*

▧ When you notice yourself feeling impatient, fearful, dis-connected, or resentful, what are the beliefs at work?

▧ What unconscious "shadow" beliefs have you become aware of over the past year? What impact have they had on your work in groups?

▧ What physical sensations are your "early warning signals" to the possibility that you have been triggered in a meeting? What do these symptoms indicate you might be feeling?

▧ What early experiences in your life make you particularly vigilant (even subconsciously) and easily triggered by cer-tain group dynamics or group member behavior?

TRY THIS

Make a list of the kinds of people, events, or situations that trigger a strong emotional reaction in you. Describe the precipitating event, the emotion that is triggered within you, and the kinds of behaviors you are prone to when acting on this emotion. Next to each hot button, make a note about any beliefs you have that support the emotional response. Think back to any life experiences during which the justifying belief might have been devel-oped or reinforced. Finally, identify alternative ways to interpret the precipitating event that might result in a different emotional response. Here's an example:

Precipitating event: A meeting participant cries.

Emotions I feel: Sadness, embarrassment, and anxiety.

Beliefs that justify the emotions: Tears always mean suffering. Tears are an abandonment of a rational process. It is my job to prevent or stop the suffering and irrationality.

Behaviors when acting on the emotion: Try to make the person feel better by providing sympathy. Pretend it is not happening and move on with the agenda. Ask the crying person if he or she wants to take a break.

Formative experiences: Parents did not approve of crying or other open expressions of emotion. Got laughed at as kid when I cried in the classroom. Societal messages that men should rescue women from their tears and make them feel better.

Alternative interpretation: This is a capable person who is feeling a very strong emotion. The tears mean this must be very important to him or her.

STAND IN THE HERE AND NOW

It's almost like I'm in an altered state of being. I am so in tune with the group that my personal thoughts and opinions—my internal dialogue—become very quiet.

—Sera Thompson

Process Facilitator

THE WORK OF LEADING GROUPS through difficult terrain can be overwhelming. Events move quickly. Voices are raised. It's easy to feel inundated. Our thoughts can begin to wander to, *What happened just now?* or, *What's going to happen?* The next thing we know, we're not really in the meeting.

How do we stay in the present moment and avoid being distracted by thoughts of the past or future? Being present connects us to ourselves and to what's happening around us. It sets the stage for us to see a difficult situation with fresh eyes, to make choices that are unclouded by emotion, and to feel an authentic sense of calm in the midst of a group storm. When we are able to draw on our present self, we can make the ongoing adjustments required to place our full attention in the here and now. Learning to be present in the fire begins with accepting the idea that the only place from which we can influence the future is in the present moment.

How Do We Burn Ourselves?

Our brains produce thousands of thoughts per day. If you take some time to notice your thoughts, you'll see that many of them are connected to regrets about the past or worries about the future.

We get into trouble when we closely identify with these kinds of thoughts and emotions. Our minds work hard to convince us that our regrets and worries are legitimate. When we get carried away in our regrets, we weaken our ability to stand with clear intention and in service to the group.

REGRETS ABOUT THE PAST

In the face of things not going as anticipated, it's easy to focus on what we should have, could have, or would have done had we only had more foresight, more insight, or more skill. Regrets come in many flavors. Our interviewees described two common ones:

> I should have anticipated this issue coming up, and now it was really disrupting the meeting.
>
> A more competent leader would have handled the moment differently than I just did.

When our thoughts about the past trigger disappointment and blame, we are living in the past, and this energy is unlikely to have any kind of positive impact on the group.

The past can teach us important lessons, but thoughts about it are useful only to the extent that they are applied in the present situation. For example, I might notice that members of the group become anxious whenever the topic of financial resources comes up. It's happened in two meetings, and I see that it is happening right now. I can regret or resent this, or I can recognize the pattern and help the group move beyond its nervousness.

WORRYING ABOUT THE FUTURE

Any thoughts about the future that do not strengthen our capacity to be in service to the group are harmful. When we get ahead of ourselves, predicting what might occur, we take ourselves out of the present—the only place where we can actually have a positive influence. Here is an example provided by a leader we interviewed. "As the task force continued its stalemate, I could see that the group was not going to achieve what we'd hoped to during this meeting. My mind started to wander anxiously to how this might impact our future meetings and my credibility as a facilitator."[1] Worries like these remove us from the present and imprison us in a world that doesn't currently, and may never, exist.

THE IMPACT OF BEING ABSENT

When our thoughts transport our consciousness into the past or future, we cannot serve our purpose in the group—to hold space for productive deliberations, collaboration, and shared commitment. In our distracted state, we are less equipped to be an instrument of change. We are less alert to what is happening, less flexible in our responses, less open to new ways of seeing challenges, and less grounded in our own purpose. We are more susceptible to acting impulsively on regrets or worries and thus likely to appear anxious or aggressive. This can undermine the group members' sense of safety as well as their view of us as trustworthy partners. In addition, our worry can spread like a virus into the group's emotional field. As discussed earlier, because of the role we play, our emotional state has a marked impact on others.

What Does It Mean to Stand in the Here and Now?

As adults, we occasionally get glimpses into what it means to be truly present in the moment. This kind of presence can happen in times of great joy—while we're feeling moved by a piece of music or a magnificent sunset—and also in times of sadness—while we're sitting with a loved one during his or her final hours of life, fully experiencing each moment because of its potential to be the last.

Standing in the here and now involves being simultaneously fully awake and totally relaxed. When we are present, we are completely aware of the flow of events as they play out from moment to moment. We have a sense of deep focus and wide vision. Time slows down and nothing outside of "right now" exists.

In the practice of tai chi, one of the first poses a student learns is called *wu chi*, which according to instructor Linda Myoki Lehrhaupt can be translated into "the mother of all possibilities."[2] In this pose one is resting still and silent, but completely alert and ready for whatever is about to unfold. Standing in the here and now creates this readiness.

It's impossible to be present all the time. Being in the here and now is more like continuously falling away from the present moment (into thoughts about the past and future) and then returning to the present. My experience with a national organization of rabbinic leaders demonstrates how high-heat meetings bring moment-to-moment challenges to stay present. The group had been convened to discuss a very divisive and emotional topic—intermarriage. An attempt twenty-five years earlier to address this topic had been seen by many as a failure, fragmenting the movement and driving the topic into the realm of the "undiscussible."

I knew that there would be a good deal of skepticism and anxiety in the first meeting. I also knew that because I am Jewish and married to a non-Jew, facilitating such a high-profile deliberation on this topic was fraught with potential hot buttons for me.

At one particular moment during an initial meeting, the debate became intense. Some of the rabbis stood up, made impassioned speeches, and took hardened positions. During those moments I worried, "This process is going to melt down into another nasty debate about right and wrong." I noticed myself resenting the people making speeches and felt the muscles in my hands tightening around the whiteboard markers. Then I remember saying to myself, "Larry, this is the second day of a three-year process. Be with them right now and breathe."

Sometimes the best we can do in these moments is to coax our attention back to the present by reminding ourselves that what has occurred cannot be reversed and that what might happen in the future has not yet occurred. The only thing that's real is what's happening right now, so that's where we need to be.

What Capacities Must We Cultivate to Stand in the Here and Now?

We can cultivate a number of abilities to help us assert and reassert our "here-ness" from moment to moment. Foremost among them are *attention* and *stillness*, especially when escaping to thoughts of the past or future represents a convenient and all-too-familiar default reaction.

ATTENTION

Attention is the capacity to simultaneously notice what is arising within us as well as around us. The key to attention is realizing this simple but powerful idea: *I am not my thoughts and emotions.*

What we think and how we feel, in any given moment, is not who we are. The mind plays tricks on us and tries to persuade us to act on our regrets and worries. As the spiritual teacher Eckhart Tolle writes, "The compulsion arises because the past gives you an identity and the future holds the promise of salvation, of fulfillment in whatever form. Both are illusions."[3] He points out that regrets about the past and anxieties about the future are seductive constructions of the mind. We all want to be "right" about the past, and we all long for a future in which our success and fulfillment are guaranteed. But when we are dwelling only in our memories and preoccupations, we are not doing the work we've been called to do.

Attention enables us to keep tabs on the internal chatter that undermines our ability to operate in the here and now. When we attend to our mental and emotional states, we take the necessary care to monitor what's happening within us. So when we notice anxiety arise, we might ask, "What's going on with me right now?" Asking might help us locate a worry about the direction in which the meeting might be heading. In that moment, we can acknowledge the concern without giving it the emotional power of a negative prediction.

Likewise, we might notice a feeling of impatience or disappointment. Again, attending involves asking, "What's going on with me right now?" A brief exploration of this question might help us realize that we are regretting a choice we made at the outset of the meeting that is now having an impact on the group's progress. Simply naming the thought often enables us to move beyond the mood of disappointment. Once we learn to recognize the over-activeness of our minds, particularly the negative chatter, we can begin to learn to quiet the internal dialogue that does not serve us. We don't cease to think. Instead, we locate the volume knob in our heads and learn to modulate it.

Here's the magic of attention: as soon as you notice that you are not in the present, you are! Paying attention is the moment-to-moment act of waking up and reawakening to what is happening right now. The realization that you have drifted into feeling bad about what just occurred or being scared about what might occur next brings your mind, heart, and body back into what is happening now. We learned this lesson from William Ury's story. In his meeting with the Palestinian leaders, he was able to name his worries about the possible "burial" of the Abraham Path project. Attending to a very real but not-so-useful internal narrative enabled him to avoid acting on his fears and to instead ask himself, "What's needed right now?"

Attention frees us of our self-defensive default scripts and enables us to make choices, including the choice to do nothing at all. This leads us to the second capacity for standing in the present moment.

STILLNESS

In this world of hyperactivity, it's difficult to be still. We often busy our minds with criticisms and predictions in order to feel reassured that we've got a handle on things. Likewise, we often fill the silence with lots of talking in order to demonstrate to others that we are leading. In a workshop a manager said to me, "Hey, if I'm not talking, I'm not leading." This is a pervasive belief in organizations today. Though incessant criticism, worry, talking, and activity may all feel like a familiar way of doing the job, they often undermine our ability to be in the here and now.

As facilitators, we are trained to listen well. But faced with a high-heat moment, our first reaction is "Say something, do anything!" In these situations, the choice to do nothing and say nothing is radical. The challenge of stillness is to resist the urge to act on the fears, regrets, and negative predictions that may be arising. Sometimes non-action comes in the form of a momentary pause—a kind of self-check on what is happening internally and externally. Stillness is an opportunity to ask ourselves, "What's really happening right now? How can I hold space for this conversation to unfold well?" At other times we may choose to remain silent for minutes, even hours.

Keeping still, by not taking control or imposing your will on the group, allows you to play the role of witness. In this role you can create value for a struggling group. For example, at a diversity training workshop I facilitated many years ago at a bank, one of the Caucasian participants made a comment that revealed some very racist assumptions. The moment I heard the words come out of her mouth, I wanted to jump in. I was filled with worry that others in the class, particularly people of color, would react angrily. I didn't want to see things blow up. Just as I leaned in, I looked over at Carmen, my co-facilitator, who had a lot more experience than I. She gave me a look that carried an unmistakable message—Do nothing! Say nothing! Be still! The first person to respond was an African American man who addressed the woman directly and respectfully. He spoke about the ways her words had wounded him. The Caucasian woman was shocked to learn that what she had stated as a self-apparent truth could be so hurtful and so inaccurate in anyone else's eyes. Realizing the impact she had had on the others in the room, she began to cry and then talked about being raised in the South by a racist father whose love and approval she'd always tried to win by parroting his views on everything. It was a powerful moment of insight and reconciliation. Carmen and I just stood still, and by our presence, we enabled the group members to do their work.

To stand with people who are passing through a time of intense anger, fear, confusion, or loss can be compared to the work of the midwife. Our actions in these moments matter much less than our ability to show up and accompany the group as a warm, caring companion on the journey of discovery. John Heider described this kind of stance in his book *The Tao of Leadership* when he wrote, "You are assisting at someone else's birth. Do good without show or fuss. Facilitate what is happening more than what you think ought to be happening. If you must take the lead, lead so that the mother is helped, yet still free and in charge. When the baby is born, the mother will rightly say, 'We did it ourselves!'"[4] Stillness is an invaluable capacity because it creates the pregnant state in the group out of which are born new possibilities that would not exist had we been busy filling the space with words and actions.

What Shifts When We Stand in the Here and Now?

When we are able to stand in the midst of conflict, confusion, and strong emotions in a way that feels totally present, we bring a number of important gifts to those who are struggling.

CALM

When we work with what is happening in the moment, no problems need to be fixed. In the present moment, we have choices about what to do or not do. We have not eliminated worry and regret, but we vigilantly attend to our own derailing thoughts and emotions as they occur and then return to the action at hand. This freedom from worry and regret creates a sense of calm. In the present moment, nervousness and anger fall away and we embody a sense of peace. Through our ability to show up in the here and now with a sense of inner peace and outer calm, we can help to create a container that is both safe and healing for others.

WIDE-SCREEN, HIGH-DEFINITION SENSING

When our seeing and feeling are not clouded by the mind's tricks, we see things in higher definition and with a wider peripheral view. A group struggling to find its way has many layers to be discovered. Presence enables us to see, hear, and feel what is happening in the room from different perspectives and at different levels.

When we can avoid getting caught in the ups and downs of a high-stakes conversation, our vision is liberated from the fog of unproductive thoughts. We are tuned in to what is happening around us. When we can see all of the colors and layers of the fire, and feel the different places from where the heat emanates, we have a wider array of choices available to us.

TO STAND IN THE HERE AND NOW IS TO BE UNENCUMBERED by thoughts about the past or future. When we become distracted by past disappointments or preoccupied with predictions about the future, feelings like regret, resentment, fear, and worry can lead us to act in ways that undermine our effectiveness with the group. For fire tenders, the only place to make a positive difference is here, and the only moment in which we can have a useful impact is right now. Standing in the here and now is less about staying in the present moment and more about *continuously bringing ourselves back* to the present as we notice regret and worry attempting to commandeer our consciousness.

QUESTIONS FOR REFLECTION

▧ When was the last time something in the past stuck with you as you were facilitating and aroused feelings of distraction or resentment? What impact did it have on your emotional state?

▧ What do you worry about most? How does your mind legitimize this anxiety about the future?

- Thinking about your body, what are the early warning signs that you are feeling regret, resentment, or worry?

- How do you experience the difference between thinking about your next move in a meeting and worrying that something bad is going to happen? How about the difference between reflecting on the past as a teacher versus dwelling in self-criticism or blame?

- What makes stillness a challenge for you when things heat up in your meetings?

TRY THIS

Choose a setting, preferably one with people in it. It can be your local coffee house, a park, or perhaps a dinner party. Experiment with immersing all of your senses in what is happening in the moment. First extend each of your physical senses into the space. What are you seeing and hearing? What are you feeling on the surface of your skin? What do you smell and taste? As thoughts and interpretations of what is happening come to your mind, simply notice them and move your attention back to your experience in the present.

Now notice whether you are picking up on an emotional energy. Don't try to analyze it or put words to it. Simply feel what is in the air. Just feel it. What was it like to immerse yourself deeply in the moment? How challenging was it to quiet your mind and simply let your senses experience the here and now? How might this serve you in your leadership and facilitation?

STAND WITH
AN OPEN MIND

I'm not listening with the idea of deciding

whether they are right or wrong, but trying to

see the way they construct their world.

—*Roger Schwarz*

Author, The Skilled Facilitator:

A Comprehensive Resource for

Consultants, Facilitators, Managers,

Trainers, and Coaches

THIS CHAPTER DESCRIBES THE
essential quality of *receptivity*. How do we
maintain a stance of openness and curiosity, especially when we are seeing behavior and hearing views that we find difficult
to accept? At times, the facilitator is the
only person in the room who is not closing down, rejecting alternative ways of
seeing, and losing hope of what might be
accomplished. Our ability as facilitators to
hold an unwavering stance of *not knowing*—
while maintaining a sense of inquiry and

optimism—is often the critical factor enabling a group to move beyond conflict and distress.

How Do We Burn Ourselves?

Whether as change agent, meeting host, negotiator, consultant, or facilitator, we bring expertise to the table. In fact, a good part of our identity is based on what we have studied in depth and practiced for many years. But seeing oneself as "someone who knows" carries a double edge. On the one hand, we can walk into a room with a sense of confidence in the things we hold to be true. On the other hand, we risk becoming too invested in that image of ourselves, which can lead to a lack of receptivity to other ways of seeing and knowing.

We undermine our effectiveness when we are closed down to other truths because they are different from or in conflict with ours. We undermine our ability to tap the wisdom of the group when we believe consciously or unconsciously that we have "arrived" in our knowing, when we respond as if our perceptions, judgments, and assumptions are the only useful take on reality.

A modern-day parable illustrates this point. Joe and Ethel were in their mid-eighties when Ethel became concerned that Joe was losing his hearing. Ethel knew that Joe did not believe in going to doctors and would not make an appointment. So Ethel went to the doctor to discuss her concerns. The doctor suggested to Ethel that she return home and speak to Joe at successive distances to determine just how serious the hearing problem was. "After you get an idea of how serious it is, come back and we'll figure out what to do next," said the doctor. When Ethel got home, she knew that Joe was tinkering in his workshop at the other end of the house. So she called out, "Joe, what do you want for dinner?" She listened but there was no reply. Walking into the living room and closer to Joe's workshop, she yelled, "Joe, honey, what do you want for dinner?" Still no reply. Ethel did this two or three more times, each time moving closer to where Joe was working. Finally, standing just behind Joe at the doorway of his workshop, Ethel asked in a loud voice, "What - would - you - like - for - dinner?" Joe turned to her, and looking quite annoyed, said, "Five times I've told you, chicken!" The old saying goes, "Seeing is believing." But sometimes believing is seeing. We see only those things that confirm our beliefs.

Intellectually, most of us embrace this quality of open-mindedness as a fundamental prerequisite for facilitative leadership. Most of us would say, "I am completely receptive to other perspectives." But most of us can point to times when we judged, labeled, or projected our biases onto others' ideas, and times when we became defensive when our expertise or assumptions were challenged.

THINKING WE KNOW

We do these things because we think we already know. In other words, some part of us believes it is more important to be right than to be effective. In fact, we are culturally programmed from an early age to value having answers over searching for answers. Neil Postman, an educator and writer, lamented, "Our children enter school as question marks and leave as periods."[1] When we stand with a truly open mind, we become question marks again.

Being receptive requires a willingness to say three words that in many organizations signal weakness: *I don't know.* Test your own comfort with these words by saying them out loud. Close the book for a moment and imagine yourself in a meeting. Someone looks to you and asks, "Where do we go from here?" Now, respond with those words. What do you feel and notice in your body as you say them? What is your posture like? How do you think others view you in this moment?

It's not what we don't know that gets us into trouble. It's what we think we know. In the workshops I teach on this topic, I often ask people to take a personal inventory of the things they think they know that get them into hot water as they lead groups. Here's a partial list. See if you can add some of your own.

I know what he or she is thinking.

I know what's best for the group.

I know what you mean.

I know what the group's options are.

I know exactly where this is going.

I know this will never work.

Our sense of certainty about our perceptions, judgments, and beliefs sneaks up on us all the time. We are more likely to get burnt when we think we know than when we admit what we don't know. We are more likely to get burnt when we allow our desire to win, to be right, and to be superior sneak up on us and we close our minds to what others have to offer.

A case in point: On one of the first consulting assignments of my career, I was sent to New York to facilitate an organizational restructuring process for a long-haul trucking company. To say I was nervous is an understatement. I was in the back seat of the cab en route to the client's office, poring over my notes and trying to reassure myself that I was prepared. Unfortunately, the cab driver wanted to chat. He was about my age, African American, dressed in a sweatshirt and torn wool cap. "What do you do for a living?" he asked. I felt annoyed and gave him a curt answer, "Consulting." He asked, "What kind of consulting?" Again, I tried to keep it short, hoping that he would get the hint. "It's called organizational development." "Ah!" he answered. "You're an OD consultant." I wondered how he knew that we refer to ourselves as "OD consultants," but I looked down at my notes and tried to refocus on my preparation. No luck. He pressed further. "So, what kind of project are you working on here in New York?" I tried to answer in layman's terms, "I'm helping a company reorganize." He responded almost instantaneously, "Oh, so you're probably drawing on some of the insights of Galbraith and Mintzberg. Is your client considering a matrix structure?" I looked up from my notes and could see him grinning in the rearview mirror. I closed my notebook, smiling for the first time that morning, and asked, "OK, who the hell are you, and why are you driving a cab?"

It turned out the cab driver had earned a master's degree in organizational studies from Yale. He had worked for one of the largest, most prestigious consulting firms in the world (the same firm that had rejected me after a single interview) and then decided that life in a large consulting firm was not for him. He invested in a small fleet of taxis and got behind the wheel every few weeks to learn more about customer needs. For the remainder of the drive, my taxi driver schooled me on many aspects of my work. He was probably responsible for any success I had with my client that day.

When we fail to remember that our teachers are all around us, we are sleepwalking through life. To stand with receptivity is to welcome the possibility that every person and every event—especially if unanticipated or uncomfortable—offers us a gift on our journey of lifelong learning.

When we fail to stand with an open mind, fully receptive to and curious about what is happening, we diminish our ability to help the group's best thinking and healing to emerge. When we are less than open-minded or too invested in our own knowing, here's what can occur:

▨ We miss out on hearing an important insight.

- We lose opportunities to learn and improve our craft.

- We become defensive when our knowledge or choices are challenged.

- We inhibit others from describing their "truth" on any given issue.

- We try to manipulate others in an attempt to validate our assumptions.

- We encourage win/lose, either/or conversations in which people are either right or wrong.

- We believe our own predictions and can become pessimistic or resigned when things are not going well.

How do we embody a spirit of openness and inquiry, especially during times when we want desperately to rely on our own knowing as a source of safety and certainty?

What Does It Mean to Stand with an Open Mind?

When we stand with receptivity to what is unfolding in the group, we must be willing to release our hold on our own certainty and say these three words: *I don't know.* Receptivity requires of us a willingness to experience the discomfort that occurs when there is a gap between our "truth" and that of others. Fundamentally, standing with this kind of openness involves deciding that it is more important to be of service than to be correct or comfortable.

The key to standing with an open mind is to declare our own ignorance and to become like constant beginners. Peter Senge, an MIT professor and the founder of the Society for Organizational Learning, wrote, "People with a high level of personal mastery are acutely aware of their ignorance, their incompetence, their growth areas. And they are deeply self-confident. Paradoxical? Only for those who do not see that 'the journey is the reward.'"[2] The journey to which Senge refers to is the journey of becoming.

Standing with an open mind as we face the fire of conflict involves creating space for contradictions to coexist. This means learning to live with our discomfort and uncertainty. The educator Parker Palmer describes this as patiently "holding the tension of the opposites."[3] He says that we need to learn to resist the urge to resolve them too quickly, allowing those tensions to "pull us open" into new insights and paths of action. This kind of tension holding is an important part of fire tending—bringing a spirit of receptivity into space filled with polarization and defensiveness.

Open-mindedness is not a state at which we arrive. It is a continuous process of opening and reopening to the limits of our own seeing and knowing, to the coexistence of ideas that appear to be incompatible, and to the possibilities arising as the conversation in the room unfolds. We open to the soft voices, the invisible stakeholders, the outrageous proposal, and the convoluted question.

You know you are standing with full receptivity when you notice yourself becoming curious about ideas that repel you. You know you are taking an open stance in the fire when, even in the most difficult moments, you are holding an infinite range of possibilities about what might be accomplished. You are being receptive when the conversation you are having with yourself sounds like "I don't need to be right about this. I'm here to learn and facilitate others' learning."

What Capacities Must We Cultivate to Stand with an Open Mind?

To stand with openness in the face of a group's fire means learning to cultivate the capacities of *embodying humility, suspending judgment, expressing curiosity*, and *holding possibility*. Each of these capacities is described below.

EMBODYING HUMILITY

Humility is not the "aw shucks" self-deprecating, falsely modest, submissive stance that many of us associate with the word. Think of humility as the sustained embodiment of a basic belief: *What I see and know is only a part of the total picture*. Cultivating this mindset involves taking on our delusion that the way we see any given situation is fundamentally comprehensive and unbiased.

It is liberating to walk into a volatile group situation knowing that we do not have to be smarter or more capable than everyone else in the room. We become alert and open to the counsel of those around us. If we are open and wise enough to ask the opinions of the group, their intuition, courage, and clarity can be the difference between harnessing the power of group fire and having things burn to ashes.

One way I remind myself about humility is to bow when I enter a meeting room. A jazz drummer and spiritual teacher named Jerry Granelli taught me this. Jerry explained that the bow represents our humility before the larger world and the group. It is what martial artists do before entering the *dojo*, the place of learning. In martial arts traditions, bowing deeply involves exposing the top of your head to another—the ultimate act of vulnerability and respect. The bow is hardly noticeable to anyone else, but it is a powerful way to remind myself that I am in the presence of people who possess their own hard-earned expertise, innate wisdom, shared aspirations, and the courage to gather to do difficult work.

SUSPENDING JUDGMENT

A second important capacity that enables us to stand fully open in the fire is the ability to suspend limiting judgments. MIT professor Otto Scharmer calls the voice of judgment "the enemy that blocks the gates to the open mind."[4] The task here is to learn to distance ourselves from our habitual ways of labeling, dismissing, interpreting, and rejecting what we hear and see.

It's useful to look at one of the original meanings of the word *suspend:* to exclude from privilege for a period of time. That definition suggests that we can give our judgmental self a time-out. When we suspend judgment, we give ourselves the mental space to notice and test a hypothesis. In this space we can ask ourselves:

What is behind my way of seeing this?
What other ways might there be to see this?
What's behind the other person's point of view?

I had to learn to suspend my judgment about tears. Early in my life I developed the habit of judging tears as bad, something to be suppressed. My ingrained judgment was that crying people needed to be comforted—and stopped. Tears were disruptive, distracting, upsetting, and certainly not in any way productive in a deliberation. Then one day I was eating lunch at a restaurant with my colleague Sherri. We were having a disagreement, and I was taken by surprise when she began to cry. I was thinking, "Did I cause it? Is anyone in the restaurant noticing? How do I make her stop now?" I then felt myself become resentful that Sherri had put me in that awkward position. I felt my anxiety turn into impatience and noticed my compassion melting away. I thought I knew the meaning of Sherri's tears.

Then she gave me a great gift that I will always cherish. She said, "Larry, when I cry it doesn't mean that I am in distress. It means that what we are talking about is important to me." She explained that there was nothing I needed to do to fix her tears—just lean in and pay attention.

This was a powerful lesson about learning to suspend my habitual judgments. I thought I knew the meaning of tears. Now I realize I don't. So I ask. Sometimes my hypothesis about crying is right and sometimes it's not. Suspending my judgment about tears enables me to be with people who are crying, in a way that's useful to them and to the group.

CURIOSITY

When we feel annoyed, defensive, or confused, it's useful to become curious about what is happening—both in the group and inside us. In modern Western society we place great value on knowing more and knowing better than others. We come to believe that those who know—those who have the answers—are superior. We are also taught to believe that those who do not possess answers or who express uncertainty in their viewpoints are somehow inferior. All this comes from the assumption that there is such a thing as certainty and that the future can be predicted.

Curiosity begins when we value not knowing. This mindset is the key to creativity and discovery. Instead of looking for evidence to support our opinions, we look with fresh eyes. Instead of defending our interpretations, we ask questions. The more we learn to live with not having the answers, the more curious we become and the more we can respect and welcome the struggles that groups face.

To be truly curious, particularly as a leader, can feel risky. It's not easy to ask questions that nobody else is willing to ask, or to challenge the status quo. It can feel terrifying to inquire into perspectives that you know may turn your own thinking upside down or inside out. But those are the choices we make to build our capacity for curiosity.

Sometimes being curious is difficult. I once piloted a town meeting process with the board of a professional association. The intention was to use this process at the association's regional membership meetings. At the conclusion of the pilot, I met with participants and asked for their feedback. The first person to speak began by providing his credentials as a process designer, strategic planner, and facilitator. He criticized both my design and facilitation at length and in a tone that I could tell was causing others to feel uncomfortable. I could feel myself closing to his suggestions, thinking, "This guy is grandstanding and trying to make me look bad so he can look good. He's got nothing of value to say." My face felt like it was on fire. I was worried that with each comment he made, I was losing professional credibility in the eyes of the group.

I had to work extra hard to become curious about his point of view. I pulled out a pen, leaned forward, and took notes so that I could get physically engaged with the value of his comments. I asked questions, and each time he replied, I consciously paused to consider what had been said. I asked others what they agreed or disagreed with. I noticed that the more curious I got about his opinions, the less adamant he became and the less defensive I felt. Soon, we were talking to each other like colleagues, and I was getting very helpful feedback.

This experience taught me a useful lesson about engaging one's curiosity while under direct fire. The moment I was able to locate my curious self, I became a tender of the fire and came back into alignment with my purpose.

HOLDING POSSIBILITY

The final capacity needed to stand with an open mind has less to do with our openness to others' ideas and perspectives and more to do with remaining fully available to hope and possibility in the fire of resistance, bewilderment, resignation, and cynicism.

Many of the most seasoned facilitators with whom I spoke during the research for this book talked about working with diverse groups of people, some of whom were sworn enemies in war or on opposite sides of a political or social issue. These stakeholders often arrived with a cynicism based on their history of failing to find common ground with one another, seeing agreements dissolve, and feeling betrayed.

For example, Marianne Hughes leads the Interaction Institute for Social Change, a consulting practice that works exclusively with leaders who are tackling complex and challenging social issues. She describes what it is like and how she must be the *steward of possibility* in this kind of setting. "It takes so much energy to hold the center on the belief that this is going to work. We know it because we've seen it work. They don't know it because they've never seen it go well."[5]

Being stewards of possibility doesn't mean that we face the fire wearing rose-colored glasses. Instead, we put adversity in its proper perspective. As others express their fears, doubts, and sense of being overwhelmed in the face of a seemingly insurmountable task, we can guide them toward taking the first small but scary steps.

To hold possibility we need to attribute the causes of failure or adversity to temporary and specific factors. We don't need to persuade anyone else in the room not to be cynical or resigned. We merely have to carry ourselves and facilitate the process with a clear spirit of optimism and possibility. Others will see it and feel it. They may label it as "unrealistic" or "idealistic," but when we are open, these labels are acceptable because we know they represent others' truths in the moment.

As a result of holding possibility, we feel more relaxed and energized even in the most challenging of moments. Over time, our ever-present expectation of a positive outcome can be contagious. Our persistent belief that there is light on the other side of the door becomes a self-fulfilling prophecy.

What Shifts When We Stand with an Open Mind?

Leaders and facilitators who stand in the fire with an open mind can help shift a group toward greater *creativity*, *safety*, and *learning*.

CREATIVITY

When we stand in judgment and certainty, we are more likely to reinforce old patterns in ourselves and in the groups with which we work. But when we adopt a mindset of not knowing, we are no longer spending energy defending our interpretations and looking for evidence to support our opinions. We are able to engage others and their ideas with fresh eyes. This kind of receptiveness creates a blank canvas for others to engage in creative thought, experimentation, and discovery. With an open mind we are more likely to hear nuances, see new patterns, and combine ideas in ways that we might overlook, discount, or resist if we are busy defending our status as someone who has the answers.

SAFETY

When we are open, people feel invited to share their perspectives. They see that although they may be challenged with rigorous questions, those questions are not aimed at making anyone feel wrong or inferior. They trust that their contributions, no matter how controversial, will be respected and valued. Standing with this kind of receptiveness is a powerful way to show people with minority views that they will be given as fair a hearing as anyone else.

LEARNING

Not surprisingly, an open mind results in the easy acquisition of new insights and learning. Humility, curiosity, and the suspension of judgment make us more permeable to life's lessons. When we view the people we are serving as potential teachers, we guarantee that we will learn from them. They teach us to be better leaders and more skillful facilitators. When we believe that every group breakdown holds the possibility of new insights and learning, then every difficult meeting informs our growth and the healthy development of the larger system.

WE BURN OURSELVES WHEN WE TOO STRONGLY identify with our own judgments as the only or best "truth" in the room. Standing with an open mind demands that we take on our need to be right, to win, to be smart and superior. It requires that we adopt a mindset that *what I see and know is only a small piece of the total picture*. When we can face the fire of people challenging our competence and expertise with a spirit of receptivity and inquiry, we change the spirit of the whole room. When we can stand with curiosity and optimism in a room filled with self-righteousness and cynicism, we are doing the transformational work of fire tending.

QUESTIONS FOR REFLECTION

- Describe the last time an important assumption or belief of yours turned out to be wrong. What did you learn?

- Have you ever thought to yourself or said to a group you were leading, "I'm not sure what's happening here," or, "I don't know where to go from here"? What did you feel? What internal dialogue was connected with these feelings?

- In what kinds of circumstances do you tend to feel a sense of self-righteousness, defensiveness, or superiority?

- When were you able to tap in to your own curiosity in the face of disturbing or confusing contributions from participants?

- Do you find it easy to hold possibility in a room filled with people who are expressing cynicism, fear, despair, or resignation? What helps you to be the steward of possibility in such moments?

TRY THIS

Tune in to your most despised radio or television political commentator, the person whose views really get under your skin. Sit down and listen for thirty minutes and notice what you feel. Listen to your judgments. Feel the emotions and physical sensations that well up. Now get curious about what this person thinks and why. What if you didn't try to prove those opinions right or wrong? If you really wanted to understand what makes this commentator tick, what questions would you ask?

KNOW WHAT YOU STAND FOR

My orientation establishes the field so that

when I am standing in the fire and a choice

point comes up, it informs or reveals a range

of choices that I might not otherwise see if

I did not have a clear orientation.

—Doug Silsbee

Leadership Coach and Author,

Presence-Based Coaching

AS THE PRECEDING CHAPTERS suggest, we are creatures of habit. But we are also creatures of choice. In the disorienting swirl of group conflict and confusion, we need to know where our feet are planted. As we face what feels like overpowering pressure to comply with a group's wishes, we need to know who we are at our core. As we feel ourselves succumbing to the pull of ego and pride, we need a higher, authentic self that serves as a solid anchor point from which to make good choices.

Every high-heat moment presents an opportunity to choose where we place our attention and how we use our considerable power as conveners. This chapter describes how knowing what we stand for enables us to choose to lead with consistency, integrity, and resolve in the face of pressures to act from self-defensive habit.

How Do We Burn Ourselves?

Defensive responses are normal default reactions. Because default reactions are connected to deeply embedded experiences and thought patterns, we engage in these behaviors without a lot of conscious thought. They are automatic. You politely suggest that I'm losing control of the meeting, and my default reaction is to explain to you why I am managing things just fine. You yell at me, and if I'm not rooted in my higher purpose, I may very well yell back.

When was the last time you left a meeting thinking any of the following thoughts?

I really didn't play the role I'd intended to play.
I lost my composure.
I got seduced by the group's belief that I could [fill in the blank].

Group fire is fraught with opportunities to make ineffective and low-integrity moves in the heat of the moment. We come face-to-face with our egos, ambitions, attachments, and fears. You might be standing in the intense heat of conflict or aggression. People in the group start to get nasty with one another. You think to yourself, "I need to keep things on an even keel here," or, "If this escalates much more, people may start to question my competence." In these moments, we want to preserve the psychological safety of the group members, and perhaps more pressingly, we want to maintain our own idealized image of ourselves as competent and in control. But acting on either of those needs—intervening in an attempt to make the heat dissipate—may not be what's needed in the moment.

Or perhaps you are working with a group that is "stuck," and you feel a mounting sense of uncertainty and fear about what to do next. You think, "How do I get these folks out of this hole they've dug?" or, "What must they think of me as I stand here so clearly not knowing what to do?" Such thoughts might lead you to take actions that reinforce the group's belief that you are in charge of making things better. Or perhaps you think, "These folks are so invested in their old victim story, I'm not sure anyone can help them." As your attention moves toward blaming the group members, you notice yourself becoming more and more resigned to what is happening, giving up on the group. These thoughts lead you to feel more comfortable and less responsible for any role you may be playing in the struggle that's occurring. But they are of absolutely no help to the group.

Too often we allow ourselves to get burnt because we are operating out of the very human and usually unconscious wish to protect ourselves. When I go into a default defense-based reaction, I am not responding to the fire from a place of clear intention or service to the group. Those are the meetings I almost always look back on and say to myself, "My most helpful, most clear, most decisive self didn't show up today." Those are the moments in which my energy became indistinguishable from the group's energy—stuck, confused, hostile, hopeless, or fearful.

In the absence of a clear sense of what we are there to contribute and what the principles are that must inform our choices, we run the risk of making a move from a purely reactive place. Here are the most common ways we typically get into trouble when we are standing in the fire without a clear guiding intention:

- Allowing individuals' emotions, power, or agendas to move the meeting away from its stated goals

- Putting on a false persona to appear more in control, more credible, and more likable

- Overreacting or too assertively intervening in ways that we later regret

- Feeling lost or distracted and thus failing to act at a time when a more assertive intervention is required

- Growing ambivalent about our involvement and questioning our ability to create value for the group

When we are leading, comfort and convenience can't be our compass points. We need a way of orienting ourselves that is connected to something more compelling than self-protection and more inspiring than self-ambition. We need a point of reference that guides us in making choices that serve the group and gives us confidence to take a personal risk.

What Does It Mean to Know What We Stand For?

It's not uncommon for facilitators and change agents working in highly charged situations to feel off balance or defensive. Here's some of the language they use to describe these moments:

- "When it happened, it felt like the rug was completely pulled out from underneath my feet. I lost my sense of what I should be doing."

- "I got swept into the group's anxiety and could no longer locate myself or make judgments independent of what was happening around me."

- "I got triggered. In that moment, the boundaries melted away and I tried to rescue the group. That was a low-integrity moment for me."

Knowing what you stand for involves a commitment to act in every situation in ways that have personal integrity for you and that serve a higher shared purpose for the group. But how do we know what we stand for? We need a kind of personal gyroscope—an internal mechanism that maintains our integrity despite the disorienting events taking place around us. Developing a personal gyroscope involves knowing and committing to a *guiding intention*. Our guiding intention articulates the authentic and personal truths that steer our choices as we tend fire. A guiding intention is not only a personal navigating system but also a source of power from which resolute action can emerge with consistency and quiet strength. Your guiding intention for any meeting consists of your answers to the following questions:

What am I here to contribute in the world?
What principles guide my work?
Who am I here for?
What does the group want to achieve?
What is and is not my job in this meeting?

We need to find ways to ask ourselves these questions on an ongoing basis. A rabbi in biblical times discovered this lesson when he was making his daily journey through the gates leading into the Holy City. One day a sentry stopped the rabbi and asked, "Where are you going? Who are you here for? Why are you here?" The rabbi thought for a moment and provided the guard with the answers to his questions.

Satisfied, he signaled the rabbi to continue through the gates. But the rabbi hesitated, looked at the guard, and asked, "How much do they pay you for this work?" The guard replied, "Twenty shekels per week." After a long silence the rabbi declared, "I will pay you thirty shekels per week if you promise to stop me each day and challenge me to respond to these three questions before I pass through these gates."

Developing our capacity to stand intentionally means becoming our own sentry at the gate of our life and work. As sentry we must ask ourselves a number of important questions, and we must listen carefully to discern the deeper truths that emerge from our answers.

WHAT AM I HERE TO CONTRIBUTE IN THE WORLD?

When we know our highest purpose, we are able to answer the question, *What am I here to contribute in the world?* This is a deeply personal question and one that forms the core of our identity. The answer to this question evolves over the course of a lifetime and must come not from external expectations but from within. Parker Palmer notes, "Before I can tell my life what I want to do with it, I must listen to my life telling me who I am."[1] Practices for exploring our higher purpose from within are offered in part III.

Higher purpose is often connected to serving others or what the management philosopher Robert Greenleaf described as "servant leadership."[2] Having a purpose that is rooted in serving the larger good enables us to more easily recognize and set aside our own ego needs (financial gain, professional status, public accolades, or whatever else), face personal risks with courage, and use our power with moral integrity.

Knowing what we are here to contribute in the world enables us to put whatever is happening in the group into a larger perspective. That perspective can be an anchor and a source of calm during a group breakdown. It can be a source of strength when we are feeling uncertain or overwhelmed. A firm grounding in an authentic, service-oriented purpose also creates a greater capacity to bounce back after being triggered. In a moment of heat, simply asking ourselves, "What am I here to contribute?" helps us move from a default response to an intentional, high-integrity choice.

WHAT PRINCIPLES GUIDE MY WORK?

Our principles are our highest, most firmly held beliefs about how we want to work in, and walk through, the world. Often, the values, beliefs, and assumptions that inform our work are unconscious and therefore unspoken. In order to be grounded in principles, we must articulate what we believe about the nature of our work and who we strive to be in the work. When we are clear about our principles, we have an ideological framework that informs both the way we see events as they unfold and the choices we make from moment to moment.

Here is a partial list of the principles that ground my work and that help me when I begin to feel anxious or lost. These are not ideas I invented. They have been given to me by many teachers over many years.

- Surprises are a given. If I could predict them, they wouldn't be surprises. The specifics of any plan I go in to the meeting with are likely to become obsolete.

- The wisdom is already in the system—I simply help to create conditions through which the group's wisdom might be revealed.

- Hearing all the voices, including those with fewer numbers and less power, is essential to a creative and inclusive process.

- When people act out toward me in anger or fear, it's almost never about me. It's not personal.

- To the extent that I can embody peace and receptivity, I can be a catalyst for transformation in the room and in the larger world.

When I consciously bring these principles into my work, they inform my physical posture, voice, and words. They serve as a personal constitution, influencing how I come to every interaction and how I assert my authority in any given moment. When I am connected to my principles, I can stand with calm, clarity, and courage in just about any room, regardless of the group's temperature.

WHO AM I HERE FOR?

The third dimension of a guiding intention is specific to the particular conversation you are convening. In advance of any meeting, I ask myself, *Who am I here to serve?* This is not always an easy question to answer, and it is one I work hard to get clear about through conversations with the client as well as in the conversations I'm having with myself.

We have to keep in mind that who we are here to serve is not always the same as who hired us. Sometimes who we are here to serve is not even in the room. Conversation host Chris Corrigan works with an organization that benefits children. To remind him and the group who they are there to serve, they often meet while children are in the room. Chris notes, "Even if the children do not participate, their presence keeps us aware and accountable."

When we are clear about who we are here for, we avoid making choices that undermine their interest. Answering this question is not about selecting a particular constituency that we will favor in the meeting. More often it is about finding the shared interest of diverse stakeholders and deciding that we are here to assist anyone who would like to pursue that interest.

WHAT DOES THE GROUP WANT TO ACHIEVE?

If we are to serve a group, we must be clear about its purpose—both for any particular meeting and in the long run. In order to discern this we must ask, *What does the group want to achieve?* and, *How does it define success?*

People convene meetings for many reasons. They want something to change. They want to move together from point A to point B. They want to get unstuck and create something new and useful. But just because they want these things doesn't mean that they will avoid getting mired in distraction, fear, and hopelessness. Just because they brought you into the process doesn't mean they will not engage in avoidance, political maneuvering, and finger-pointing.

As a result, you need to be firmly rooted in what the group says it wants to achieve. In the midst of confusion and conflict, your ability to connect quickly with the group's purpose is essential to knowing what you stand for.

WHAT IS MY JOB AND WHAT IS NOT MY JOB IN THIS MEETING?

The fifth element of guiding intention has to do with understanding our role in a particular situation. From meeting to meeting our role might change. Grounded in our own purpose and convictions and informed by what the group wants to achieve, we need to ask ourselves two other questions that will create the most value for the group: *What is my job in this meeting? What is not my job in this meeting?*

Sometimes my role might be solely process facilitation. Other times the group may value my observations and lessons about team dynamics or skillful conversation. Both for the group and for ourselves, it's very important to gain clarity about our role in advance.

During the course of a difficult group process the boundaries of our roles can slip. Many of us are in this work because we want to serve others. That motivation can get us into trouble when we take on tasks and responsibilities that unintentionally weaken the capacity of the group to take responsibility for its own work.

Like the rabbi at the gates of the Holy City, we must ask ourselves these important questions before stepping through the doors and into a high-heat meeting. When we arrive with a clear guiding intention, we are able to face the fire knowing where we stand and what we stand for.

What Capacities Must We Cultivate to Know What We Stand For?

Clarity and *commitment* enable us to know what we stand for instead of automatically reacting in the face of tricky meeting dynamics. In order to truly know what we stand for, we must develop these two key capacities.

CLARITY

When we are clear about our guiding intention, we see things with sharpness and precision, unclouded by the external drama playing out around us or by the internal emotions we are experiencing. When we can stand in the fire fully connected to guiding intention, we can make choices in service to the group and be true to our own integrity.

Clarity about our guiding intention is especially essential in high-stakes conversations. The internationally recognized negotiator William Ury told me about being sent by Jimmy Carter and the Carter Center to meet with President Hugo Chavez of Venezuela in 2005. "Venezuela was on the brink of a bloody civil war, and I was told I would have fifteen minutes with Chavez and members of his Cabinet," Ury recalls. Just before the meeting Ury went to the garden courtyard of his Caracas bed and breakfast to reflect on his guiding intention. "As I sat there in the garden, I decided that I would sacrifice my opportunity to give advice and instead just listen to Chavez. I also decided that my focus would be on the children of Venezuela—preserving their ability to grow up in a peaceful country. That's where my center was, and everything I did during the meeting was guided by this." What was intended to be a fifteen-minute meeting lasted for two hours and culminated in President Chavez asking for Ury's advice and agreeing to begin talks with his "enemies." To be clear about what you stand for is to have a powerful anchoring point in uncertain and potentially turbulent interactions.

We cultivate clarity through the discipline of reflecting on the questions about our guiding intention. You will learn specific "preparation practices" related to clarifying your guiding intention in chapter 10.

COMMITMENT

Commitment represents a deep personal conviction about our guiding intention. If *clarity* means intellectually knowing what we stand for, *commitment* is aligning with our guiding intention at the levels of mind, heart, and body. Commitment involves taking personal ownership of our guiding intention, even as it is evolving over time.

As indicated at the beginning of this chapter, our reactive selves are committed to maintaining our own safety and comfort. These strong, unconscious commitments result in default responses. When we commit to a guiding intention, we are making a choice that our thoughts, our actions, and our very way of being will be guided by a higher set of commitments—our guiding intention. In effect, we declare, "I choose these higher commitments over my habitual way of responding."

Our commitments not only guide us in what we say yes to but also inform us when we need to say no to others and to ourselves. As a result of the commitments I make to myself, I more often say no to my own defensive tendencies. I say no to leaders who want to hold meetings in order to create the illusion of inclusion rather than the real thing. I say no to my own desire to stick with the agenda when something else is emerging that the group wishes to address.

Committing to a guiding intention before we step into a high-heat meeting is like taking a sacred warrior's vow before going into battle. We decide who we want to be and who we are there to serve, knowing that there will be forces that might seduce us away from our higher self. Committing is more than just believing something to be true. It is a deep *knowing*—a trust in our internal gyroscope that enables us to make choices from the solid foundation of our truth.

What Shifts When We Know What We Stand For?

When we can stand with a deep connection to our guiding intention, people see it. They experience a leader who is resolute—not easily distracted by the emotion of the moment or weighed down by the struggle. They sense that we make choices and take actions that are informed by our principles. Our clarity and commitment to a guiding intention conveys to others a grounded presence that helps them connect with what they themselves want to stand for.

As we cultivate our ability to stand in the fire guided by our guiding intention, we and others will experience three powerful shifts.

COHERENCE

When we are rooted in our guiding intention, we embody internal consistency. Our words, our actions, and our very being form a unified whole when we are aware of and connected to what we stand for. The more we work at clarity and commit to what is important, the more we gain a sense of internal coherence—personal alignment and integrity. We feel that we are drawing on all the best parts of ourselves. Saint Francis of Assisi said, "It is no use walking anywhere to preach unless you are walking your preaching." We achieve personal coherence when we are "walking" our guiding intention. As people witness this kind of integrity in action, they are more likely to trust the credibility and consistency of our actions. They relax into the process.

COURAGE

Courage is not the absence of fear. It is our willingness to step toward something scary in spite of our fear because we feel compelled to action by a higher purpose. Knowing what we stand for connects us to something larger than our need to look good or to simply survive a difficult meeting. It helps us identify with a higher calling that is more important than comfort.

Taking a courageous stand for what we believe in need not involve aggression. Aggression simply produces aggression. A well-honed guiding intention enables us to bring a consistently peaceful yet firm resolve to difficult interactions.

Courage has a contagious quality through which others discover the common good for which they are inspired to stand.

AUTHENTICITY

As we commit to and embody our guiding intention, we are less susceptible to adopting a false persona in order to get through a high-heat moment. We can resist our own self-consciousness and ambition as well as the external pressures to be someone we are not.

When we know what we stand for, we know who we are and do not feel the need to change that. In a world that seems increasingly filled with celebrity, public image, and spin, authenticity is an important source of trust and credibility.

As we embody relaxed authenticity, we give others in the group permission to do the same. And when people show up authentically, they bring the full spectrum of their experience, insights, and energy into the conversation.

> Courage is not the absence of fear. It is our willingness to step toward something scary in spite of our fear because we feel compelled to action by a higher purpose.

DISCOVERING WHAT WE STAND FOR

Knowing what we stand for means frequent encounters with our own integrity. These moments are often inconvenient and uncomfortable. Here is a personal story that illustrates how clarity and a commitment to purpose and principles enabled a sense of coherence, courage, and authenticity to emerge.

During the first month of my first job after graduate school, I was sent out with a more senior colleague to meet with a prospective client— a widely respected casino. The project we were pitching involved a particular area of expertise I brought to the firm, and though I was inexperienced, I was asked to take the lead on the presentation. At the conclusion of the meeting with the CEO and his senior leadership team, we were informed that they would be awarding us the consulting contract. I was elated.

As the meeting ended, the CEO offered to walk with us to our car. As we walked through the casino, I thought I might impress the CEO with a few thoughtful questions about his business. I asked, "Who is your target customer?" He said, "Great question, Larry," and I smiled, proud of myself. He continued, "Our target customer is the addictive gambler—the person who goes straight to the check-cashing service on payday and makes a beeline for our casino. At the end of the evening, they have lost a good part of their paycheck and are often so high on their own endorphins, they can't bring themselves to leave the table even to go to the bathroom." I was shocked. Seeing that I lacked a brilliant follow-up question, my colleague bid the CEO goodbye and thanked him for selecting us.

When we sat down in the car, I turned to my colleague and said, "I can't work on this project." She understood but told me that the project could not be completed without me. She suggested that I was being idealistic and naive and gently reminded me I was new to the firm, had student loans, and worked for a boss who would not be sympathetic. But I knew I had to go back to the office and inform my new boss that I could not work for a company that defined its business mission in terms of preying on people with addictions. They were clear about their mission, but I was clear about mine—to foster healthy human systems. And I was even clearer that the two could not live together.

As I explained to my boss the reasons I could not work on this project, he asked, "Is the casino doing anything illegal?" I told him that I didn't think so but that legality really wasn't the basis of my decision. He tried to be understanding, though I could tell he was annoyed. I kept thinking to myself, "If I compromise my integrity during my first month on the job, I'll be lost for the rest of my career."

In the end, my boss let me take a pass on the project, advising me, "You get one of these during the course of your career here, and this is it." As a result of my decision, the firm lost the business. I discovered that my values were different from the firm's and that I would need to make a move when the time was right. When the right moment came, I did.

That was a high-heat moment for me, but in the midst of all the risk, I remember feeling relatively calm. I felt both clear and committed to the ethical stance I was taking. This clarity and interior commitment enabled me to be faithful to my higher purpose, something that was more important than my short-term job security.

IN THE HEAT OF CONFLICT OR PRESSURE TO COMPLY with a group's wishes, we need to know who we are at our core. When we feel ourselves succumbing to the pull of ego and pride, we need to know that we stand for something more than self-protection and self-ambition. Any true fire tender will tell you that there are times when we must act with clarity and resolve, and in those moments, comfort and convenience can't be the ground we stand on. When we are rooted in our guiding intention, we are less susceptible to getting knocked over, swept away, and seduced by the group dynamic. And in those moments that we do become reactive, a clear guiding intention helps us recover more quickly and find a response that has integrity.

QUESTIONS FOR REFLECTION

■ In what situations have you felt as though you lost yourself or abandoned your purpose and belief system?

■ In what situations have you maintained your integrity and authenticity despite the pressures to abandon yourself?

■ In what kinds of situations do you tend to choose caution and comfort over making the right move? In these moments, is there a higher principle you let go of?

- Who have been the significant teachers in your life? What lessons did they teach you that inform how you see and do your work?

- What are you committed to that you would not compromise in your work? in your life?

TRY THIS

Find a quiet place to sit with a partner. Provide your partner with these three questions: (1) Who are you? (2) What have you chosen to stand for in your life? (3) What are you here to contribute in the world?

Ask your partner to spend ten minutes asking you each question. During each ten-minute period your partner's only role is to listen very carefully to your responses and then pose the same question again. He or she should make no commentary or attempt to probe deeper. After ten minutes your partner should move on to the second question, and then ten minutes later to the third.

Take an additional thirty minutes to describe to your partner what you learned. What were the more superficial, ego-driven, or socially acceptable answers you had to break through to get to deeper, more authentic statements about yourself? What was empowering about this? What was scary? What did you learn about what your higher purpose is and is not?

DANCE WITH SURPRISES

If I can't find a way to let go, it carries over into

the gathering and I become very controlling—

and I tend not to let things unfold.

—Chris Corrigan

Facilitator and Process Consultant,

Harvest Moon Consultants

A MEETING WITHOUT SURPRISES is a meeting in which nothing particularly important occurs. Without surprises we learn very little, because everything that occurs is exactly what we expected. Surprises are that disruptive spark that often lights the fire for innovation. But our human nature is such that when shocking or even merely unexpected events occur, we resent them.

When we can dance with surprises, we are able to welcome and work in concert with whatever is occurring. In the face of surprises, we embody an effortless grace and adaptability. We don't hold on to preconceived outcomes, resist unforeseen events, or resent an unanticipated change in the agenda we worked so hard to craft. When we move fluidly in the fire, we are inviting the unexpected to be our dance partner. We view every person, every event, every piece of new information, and every expressed emotion as our partner in the creation of something new.

How Do We Burn Ourselves?

The key vulnerability is our desire for control. After nearly twenty-five years of working with groups of all sizes and types, I still have to remind myself that I can't control what people say, how they say it, or what they do in a meeting. I still have to surrender to the fact that the discussion will not be as predictable, linear, and logical as I'd like it to be. I have had to accept the law of the trickster. A creature in many shamanic traditions, the trickster serves as a rather sneaky teacher. Just when we think we are on the road to achieving our goals, the trickster throws us a curve ball, a snowball, or a fur ball—something completely unexpected that we have no idea how to catch, let alone hold on to. In the context of meetings, the trickster might appear in the form of a participant who acts in ways you label "illogical" or "inappropriate." The trickster can also appear in the form of events or circumstances (perhaps a snowstorm or the illness of a key participant) that disrupt a well-honed plan. The trickster very often appears in the form of a key insight the group stumbles upon, an insight that needs more time— time you don't have.

For many years when confronted with tricksters I sought to control them—to manipulate or wrestle them into submission. Often it was I who wound up being wrestled into submission, resignation, or resentment. The more I fought to regain control, the more I lost.

Here's what happened with one anonymous facilitator when it looked as though a group wouldn't achieve everything on the agenda. "I felt frustrated with them because they did not work faster. But honestly, I was really angry with myself that I had not planned a more realistic agenda. Either way, I now know that my impatience and frustrations were visible. They got in the way of helping the group."[1]

Each of us has tricksters that have power over us—certain kinds of events and people that trigger our fears and need for control. When our most powerful tricksters appear and we want to battle rather than dance with them, we can't see things clearly and adapt to what's happening in the room. When we're focused on controlling rather than flowing, here's what happens:

- We lose our sense of humor.

- We become fixated on what is not working and on our inability to move beyond that focus.

- We give up, convinced that we can't be of help.

- We feel annoyed and resentful, blaming ourselves and others for what is happening.

- We attempt to use our expertise or authority to assert control over what people say, do, and feel.

- We stick to our plan and pretend that the unexpected moment did not occur.

Each of those responses is a very safe and natural reaction in a high-heat moment. When we get surprised, it's easy for us to dig in and become rigid, self-protective, or positional in our thinking. Each response is an indicator that we are attached to something. That something is often a belief about what should be happening. We should be able to assure the outcome of this meeting and spare participants discomfort and distress. If a plan is good, we should not have to change it. People should be more logical and less emotional. They should communicate concisely and show up on time. We should be able to quickly put things back on track when they get messy.

Here's a useful exercise: During the course of your daily routine, notice when you become impatient or lose your sense of perspective. Notice what you are feeling and thinking while you're on hold with customer service or navigating an airline's automated reservation system. Pay attention to your mood as you stand in line at the grocery store or drive on the freeway. Notice what you feel when the people in your life let you down.

Now take that trained eye into your work and begin to notice the ways in which you become inflexible in the face of an unmet expectation. What self-imposed "shoulds" do you take into your meetings and relationships?

What Does It Mean to Dance with Surprises?

Dancing with surprises means learning to be fluid and flexible in the face of unexpected events that have the potential to shake us up or knock us off our feet. It means being willing to surrender to the realities of a situation so that we can then work creatively with those realities.

Harrison Owen, the creator of Open Space Technology, calls people who have mastered the ability to dance with surprises "wave riders." He describes them as "curious people possessed of an innate capacity to go with the flow, constantly seizing upon opportunity when others see no possibility, or even disaster."[2] He asserts that wave riders do not regard lightly that which is planned, logical, or born out of hard work. In fact, they may assign great value to those qualities. What sets wave riders apart is that they understand the limitations of planning, logic, and hard work.

What Capacities Must We Cultivate to Dance with Surprises?

As the sparks of dissent begin to fly or the smoke of confusion fills the air, how do we employ the effortless grace of a dancer to respond skillfully in the moment? The kind of adaptability we need involves cultivating three capacities—*letting go*, *playfulness*, and *faith*.

Several years back I had the opportunity to work with an extraordinary business. It was an artists' cooperative founded by and consisting of formerly homeless artists. Some of them struggled with addiction and mental illness. Many had spent time in prison. I met with them in their rented warehouse "studio" space in one of the poorest and most depressed areas in downtown Los Angeles. I was invited to facilitate a strategic planning meeting involving the entire co-op membership. One of the key questions facing the organization was how to effectively promote and sell their "outsider art" to the public.

About twenty minutes into the meeting, one of the members began to giggle loudly, slap her hand on the table, and mumble something about "getting on the bus." I assumed that this was a nervous tic, and later some of the co-op leaders told me that she had a form of mental illness and had gone off her medication earlier in the week. Soon the outbursts became more frequent and disruptive. She began to sing, "Getting on the bus—yes, we are—getting on the bus." I had to work hard to move from feeling anxiety and frustration on my own behalf to feeling compassion for the woman. At the same time, I didn't want our meeting to get hijacked by one person who seemed to be having a wonderful conversation in a parallel universe.

I could not remove the woman from the room, and yet it was impossible to ignore her presence. Her table banging, laughing, and chanting was the reality on the ground, and the sooner I surrendered to it, the better. I made a quick decision to ask the artists to create some "art from the moment." I wrote on the board, "ideas for marketing our art" and invited people to join in slapping on the table and singing. In a few moments, we had quite a lively performance piece going—percussion, chanting, and yelling out ideas. The "bus lady" seemed delighted. We stopped being bothered and resentful and became celebratory and playful. And here's the best part: At the conclusion of the planning day, the group decided that the best way to market the outsider art was to buy a reconditioned school bus, decorate it, and take it to street festivals throughout the state as a mobile gallery.

I had felt I had no choice but to surrender to the facts on the ground—this woman was part of the meeting and would not be silenced. I had to let go of my original plan. In fact, I remember smiling to myself, thinking that perhaps she was the only sane one in the room and we were crazy ones trying to use a linear planning process in a warehouse on skid row. And when I asked myself, "How do you want the story to go from here, Larry?" I became playful with my thinking. That's when the music idea came to me. What enabled me to suggest such a wacky idea was my faith. I had seen them create beautiful objects out of industrial garbage and discarded materials. I knew that they could create their strategy using musical improvisation. Thanks to my willingness to literally improvise with surprises, what was a barely tolerated distraction in the morning became a moneymaking idea by the afternoon.

LETTING GO

In order to stand and move with the flow, we need to examine our attachments—the beliefs that we want to hold on to and the things we feel entitled to. Whether or not we admit it, many of us are attached to being liked and being viewed as an expert. We want to be needed. As mentioned earlier, we also become attached to certain expectations of how people should act and how things should go in our meetings. When these attachments get in the way of our adapting, they hinder our effectiveness as leaders and facilitators.

What do you clutch too tight and in a way that hinders your effectiveness? Here are some possibilities to consider:

- Beliefs about yourself, who you are, and what you should be able to do

- Expectations about how others should behave—what is "appropriate" and "inappropriate" in a particular setting

- Opinions about how fast, smooth, and according to plan things should go in the meeting

- An investment in particular outcomes

To let go is to hold these beliefs and expectations lightly and be willing to release them when it serves your guiding intention. Letting go involves first recognizing the things to which you feel attached, naming them, and then loosening your psychological grip. One facilitator we interviewed discovered he was once strongly attached to his agenda. "The more I tried to convince them of the rightness of my agenda," he said, "the more they resisted. Finally, when I realized what I was doing and expressed openness to refining the agenda, people's resistance dropped away."[3]

I had a similar experience with a group of farmers and farmworker representatives who had been invited to participate on a task force to design farmworker housing that would be built by the state. Within the first thirty minutes of the meeting, people started to bring up the long history of disappointment and betrayal. The conversation got heated, and I could feel the room dividing into two factions. I realized that the goals I'd planned with a few of the leaders in the room were not realistic. They were just not ready to have the conversations we had hoped to have.

Once I was able to let go of my need to achieve the predetermined outcomes in the meeting, lots of interesting possibilities opened up. Working during a break with the conveners of the meeting, we quickly redefined the goals and redesigned the agenda. At the outset of the meeting, I thought that throwing away my original plan would make me look weak and incompetent as a facilitator. That decision wound up doing just the opposite. The "plan B" agenda we developed during the break achieved a measure of reconciliation among the group members, enough to form a foundation for the group to ultimately reach consensus on a first-ever statewide plan for farmworker housing.

When standing in the fire of groups, most of us share a similar attitude toward failure. We believe that if we are not able to make the right move in the moment to help the group, we will be perceived as incompetent. We believe we will lose our status and credibility. We fear the group will flounder or fragment. We fear everyone will feel intensely uncomfortable and that the moment may last forever!

Letting go can help us change our attitude about failure. After all, as the leadership guru Kevin Cashman writes, "Failure is a subjective label we apply to unintended or unexpected experiences."[4] By letting go of our attachments, we can focus on more useful questions, such as, *What's needed at this moment?* and, *What lessons does this moment hold for me and this group?*

PLAYFULNESS

When we approach serious and complex topics with a playful spirit, we bring joy, fullness of participation, spontaneity, and humor to the work. Building our capacity to play means learning to view chaos, confusion, and conflict as partners rather than foes. To be playful is to approach our role with lightheartedness. We can take the work seriously, but we don't have to take ourselves too seriously.

One belief that has helped me become much more playful in my work facilitating high-stakes meetings is the notion that there is no "one right move" in any given situation—that many options will work. This belief frees me up to play creatively with ideas and the choices I can make. In the same way, as Margaret Wheatley and Myron Kellner-Rogers wrote in their book *A Simpler Way*, "Agility and the freedom to be creative are more likely when we focus on what works rather than what is right."[5]

The capacity to play is particularly helpful when you need to recover from a misstep. Perhaps you got triggered into a defensive response. Maybe you intervened in a way that created more confusion or anxiety for people. We make errors all the time, and if we can be playful with ourselves, we can smile and keep playing. Sometimes we can even use our missteps to create something great. But that also requires us to see even our mistakes as part of the art that's being created.

A colleague of mine told me about a time when she was able to use playfulness to recover after she lost her neutrality. She was facilitating a meeting in her community and when an issue came up about which she cared very deeply, she blurted out her opinion as she stood at the front of the room. It was only a momentary lapse, but she could see

> To be playful is to approach our role with lightheartedness. We can take the work seriously, but we don't have to take ourselves too seriously.

by the expression on the faces of the participants that she'd violated her agreement with the group to be impartial. Without hesitation she smiled and said, "Let's rewind this," at which point she did her best to act out in reverse what had just transpired. It got a chuckle from group members. She took a breath, apologized for momentarily stepping outside her role, and reiterated her commitment to remain neutral.

FAITH

Another capacity that enables us to move with the flow and improvise in difficult situations is faith. Faith is not necessarily unquestioning confidence in someone or something. It involves being in an active, committed inquiry about the way the world works and the beliefs that enhance and affirm life. In order to move fluidly in the face of difficult group dynamics, I have learned to place my faith in the following beliefs:

- Every time I convene a group of people is an opportunity to create the world in which I want to live.

- Breakdowns, surprises, mishaps, and messiness, which we often label "failures," are a normal part of the journey toward innovation and transformation.

- Everything and everyone is interconnected and interdependent— I am affecting others, and I am affected, in ways I am often not able to see.

- My ability to bring a wholehearted, authentic, grounded presence into a gathering space increases the likelihood that others will do the same.

How do we cultivate faith? It's not helpful to invest time trying to prove that these kinds of beliefs are empirically true or false. I suggest that as you choose what to put your faith in, you consider beliefs that enable you to be of service to groups, to keep your ego in check, and to navigate the uncertain and painful moments of fire tending. Ask yourself, *What beliefs put me into rapport instead of conflict with the challenges and mysteries of life?* Over time you will want to evaluate these beliefs, not based on their truth, but on the extent to which they enhance your ability to dance with surprises and remain a centered, life-affirming presence in the face of high heat.

What Shifts When We Learn to Dance with Surprises?

The better we become at maintaining a flexible stance during difficult moments, the more we help to shift the energy in ourselves and in those around us. When we demonstrate the ability to move with the flow, we increase the level of *agility* and *confidence* in a meeting.

AGILITY

As we practice dancing with surprises we gain agility—quickness and surefootedness—especially in the face of unexpected obstacles. Because fluidity enables us to accept difficult situations more quickly, we are able to see the choices we have more quickly and can make a skillful move or choose not to move at all. We don't get bogged down in our own resistance or resentment about what is happening. We don't waste time digging in to a position or holding tight to an expectation of how things should be. The absence of self-imposed friction enables us to adapt with speed and ease. Our quickness in adjusting enables others not to get bogged down by their own resistance.

CONFIDENCE

The more we practice dancing fluidly with surprises, the more confidence we gain in our ability to handle whatever comes our way. As we build our capacity to detach ourselves from certain expectations, to become more playful, and to choose the beliefs in which we are willing to put our faith, we become more confident as we face high-heat moments. Confidence in our ability to adapt conveys encouragement to the group, especially in moments of doubt and anxiety.

SURPRISES HAVE A WAY OF SHOWING UP UNEXPECTED, unannounced, and unwanted. They're a given in meetings. We can't prevent or control them because we can't predict them. Rather than become resentful, anxious, or distracted by surprises, we need to learn to dance with them—to invite these uninvited guests into our meeting and welcome the creative possibilities they offer. Dancing with surprises is the ability to respond with flexibility and grace as the unexpected occurs. When we can learn to approach the unexpected with playfulness and lightness, we can transform what initially felt like a breakdown into a breakthrough.

QUESTIONS FOR REFLECTION

■ When has surrendering to the realities of difficult people, behaviors, or circumstances enabled you to adapt in ways that served the group?

■ What strongly held beliefs and expectations about yourself tend to undermine your ability to be flexible?

- Who are the tricksters in your life—the people and events that have taught you about flexibility and have revealed your patterns of rigidity, judgment, and control?

- In what situations does your sense of playfulness and experimentation come out? What interior beliefs and external conditions enable this to happen?

- What beliefs enable you to overcome your fears, go with the flow, or make a bold move in your work?

TRY THIS

To what do you feel attached? To what part of your public image (say, neatness) do you feel strongly attached? To what material things (for example, books) do you feel strongly attached? To what comforts (maybe a hot shower each morning) do you feel strongly attached? To what daily or weekly routines (a morning bagel perhaps) do you feel strongly attached? Give up one of these for a week. If being neat is important, stop combing your hair before you go out. If you are attached to hot showers, turn up the cold water for a week. Notice what emotions and beliefs come to the surface. In the process, notice what other attachments you discover. For the weeks that follow this exercise, keep three lists:

- Things I need to believe about myself

- Things I need to do

- Things I think should happen

STAND WITH COMPASSION

Sometimes we guard our impartiality and professional distance at the expense of allowing compassion into our work.

—Sidney Wasserman

Professor of Social Work

BY THE END OF THIS CHAPTER I want you to be familiar with a way of standing with your heart wide open to yourself and to others. As change agents working in emotionally volatile situations, our goal is not to extinguish or become impervious to unpleasant feelings. Our goal is to learn to feel human fear and heartbreak without defaulting into a fight-or-flight mode. In this chapter we will explore how the capacities of *emotional openness, self-acceptance, awareness of the whole person*, and *unconditional positive regard* enable us to tend the fire in ways that invite human dignity into spaces where fear, intolerance, and aggression might otherwise take over.

How Do We Burn Ourselves?

Where there is group fire, there is often pain and suffering. And where there is suffering, there is nearly always the tendency for people to move into fight-or-flight reactions. Despite some older notions of the facilitator as someone "standing outside of it all," we are in fact, a very real and connected part of the system. When things heat up, we have no heat-resistant suit to slip into, nor would it serve our purpose if we did.

Despite some older notions of the facilitator as someone "standing outside of it all," we are in fact, a very real and connected part of the system.

As professionals who spend a lot of time working with groups, we know how we wish people would function when they hit rough spots. We have seen them at their best, their most collaborative, their most communicative; and it would certainly be more convenient if everyone showed up this way every time. The reality of groups is that they rarely do what we would like them to do. People get triggered into emotional reactions. Some become aggressive, others argumentative, and still others retreat into silence.

When the group dynamic becomes challenging and individuals begin to act in reactive ways, we can also become reactive. We know our hearts are closing when:

- We feel superior to others

- We feel numb to what is occurring

- We feel judgmental, impatient, or irritated with ourselves or others

- We are unkind or even hurtful toward ourselves and others

- We dismiss or ignore certain people

- We silently label people with words like *inappropriate*, *manipulative*, or *dumb*

- We decide we know someone's motives, character, or competency

- We are intimidated by or deferent to certain people

These responses diminish the kind of safety and trust we hope to create in our meetings. We know this intellectually, but our fears and judgments will kick in unless we can expand our capacity for compassion.

REPRESSION AS A WAY TO FLEE

Faced with behavior that we find annoying or problematic, one default reaction is to look for a way out. Since we are often not able to leave the room, we find ways to flee psychologically. In the name of "professional detachment" we deaden our minds and anesthetize our hearts. While some degree of psychological distancing is useful, we too often convince ourselves that total emotional detachment best serves the group in an incendiary moment.

Some of us learned to detach from emotionally intense situations at an early age. When I was growing up, I attended a school where I had to endure everyday encounters with bullies and gang members. From about fifth grade on, I would wake up each morning, stand in front of the mirror, and practice looking unafraid. I would also practice dulling my emotions—especially fear. As a kid, I found that this helped me get through the halls each day. As an adult, I learned that a similar approach was not effective in leading groups through difficulty. For many years, I facilitated group conflicts with complete detachment and an almost deadpan clinical presence.

I thought that this level of detachment was serving the group, but I came to realize how much I missed by not allowing myself to get closer to what the group was feeling. I now realize that only by taking off my emotional Kevlar and exposing myself to life's uncomfortable feelings can I help others navigate through theirs.

The repression and denial of emotions can become a form of learned *apathy*. The Greek word *apatheia* means "nonsuffering," or the inability to experience pain. Though it sounds like an appealing state, cloaking our hearts has profoundly negative consequences. Anesthetizing ourselves to the world of emotions requires a huge amount of energy and disables us from understanding what is truly happening in the room. We cannot tend the fire if we cannot feel the intensity of its heat. We cannot be in service to human struggle if we have isolated ourselves from the fundamental quality of what it means to be human.

AGGRESSION AS A WAY TO FIGHT

When things get tense, we want to resolve the tension. We attempt to turn things around with what we hope will be elegant interventions and inspiring insights. If that doesn't work, we try to put things on an even keel through forms of overt aggression, such as argumentative language and facial expressions, including frowning and rolling the eyes. Blame is another form of aggression. More subtle forms of overt aggression use hurtful sarcasm or a condescending tone.

We might also express aggression covertly or passively by avoiding eye contact, manipulating people, or ignoring them. Such actions may imply a belief that someone in the group is uncooperative, illogical, or politically motivated.

Those are forms of reactive aggression. But not all aggression is negative. Aggression can also be the forceful use of energy for constructive purposes. For example, if we assert ourselves in order to remind the group of its operating agreements or intervene in a personal attack, we are engaging in a constructive and appropriate form of aggression, grounded in the integrity of the guiding intention we explored earlier.

Our hearts close against others mainly because of our projections. We are projecting when we assign our qualities, moods, and motives to other people. What we reject in ourselves, we reject in others. What we admire in ourselves, we admire in others.

We use projection to keep us blind to certain parts of ourselves we don't want to see. We might think "That person is playing politics" as a way to deny the part of us that is politically motivated or manipulative. We might decide "This is a very angry and dysfunctional person" as we deny the anger in ourselves. If we are not aware that we are projecting, the stories we create about others can quickly carry us into negative stances like distrust and arrogance.

What Does It Mean to Stand with Compassion?

One of our biggest challenges in the fire is to remember that we all struggle with uncertainty, contradictions, ambiguity, and pain as we search for collective wisdom and common ground. In our work we encounter people that we might label mean-spirited, arrogant, resistant, disrespectful, cynical, or evil. Standing with compassion means that we acknowledge the struggle and suffering within people. Even as they are not living up to our expectations, we recognize our own struggle in theirs.

The Hebrew word for compassion is *rachamim*, which shares the same linguistic root as the word *rechem*, meaning "womb."[1] In this light, "compassion" suggests the human connection and tenderness associated with motherhood. It is a connection that transcends physical separateness and that even in the most difficult times enables us to draw on our capacity for forgiveness and kindness.

Compassion does not preclude us from confronting behaviors and challenging people in ways that may stretch their comfort zone. In fact, compassion sometimes requires this of us. Nor does it mean pitying people. Feeling sorry for people only amplifies any sense that they are victims and we are rescuers.

Before we can extend compassion to others, we must learn compassion for ourselves. It is possible to extend a fully open heart to others only if we are able to recognize and stop self-aggression, self-hate, and self-directed blame. We are less likely to inflict on others what we are unwilling to inflict on ourselves.

Leading with compassion transforms our way of seeing and being. We can see a situation with compassion, or with aggression. And those two ways of seeing will affect the kind of resource we become for the group.

I had to transform my way of seeing from aggressive to compassionate when a colleague and I were facilitating a leadership training session on how to have Fierce Conversations.[2] Early in the session three men seated together began to talk critically and loudly about the futility of such a course. "Yeah," one said, "if I have a candid conversation with my boss, I'll need to start working fiercely on my résumé because I'll be looking for a new job." Very quickly, I began to see these men as my adversaries. I convinced myself that I needed to stop them from wrecking my workshop. Outwardly, I tried to laugh off their jokes and encourage them to try the ideas on for size before dismissing them. But I know that my impatience was apparent in my tone and on my face.

During the first break, I asked my co-facilitator what we were going to do about those problem participants. I was shocked to hear her response: "What problem participants? I love the fact that they are being so candid during a workshop about candor." All morning I had felt defensive and resentful about those guys. And all morning my colleague was feeling delighted with their candor and openness about their doubts. We were in the same room, but we had a completely different take on what was occurring.

When I came back into the room, I watched my colleague inquire into the fears and doubts of those expressing skepticism. Soon others began to express similar worries. I remembered my own struggles speaking up to people in authority and was able to share some of those with the group. Within an hour, people seemed excited to get on with the training. They'd felt reassured that all of their fears, hopes, and concerns had been heard. I had acknowledged their humanity and in doing so, remembered my own.

As we experience the struggles of others, we recognize our own journey of pain and suffering. And in that journey we discover toler-ance, acceptance, and fulfillment. Along the way we become less and less susceptible to our default reactions—disliking, ignoring, blaming, idealizing, resenting, and rescuing others.

What Capacities Must We Cultivate to Stand with Compassion?

Learning to stand with compassion is a lifelong endeavor. Just when we think we are the embodiment of open-heartedness in our life and work, a new, challenging person walks into the room and reminds us of those aspects of ourselves with which we still struggle. The capacities that help us to stand with compassion are the most challenging in this book because we can't think our way into them. They require that we allow ourselves to feel things that our most human instincts want to protect us from.

EMOTIONAL OPENNESS

Developing our capacity to be emotionally open means taking off a lifetime's armor of self-protective strategies. During his interview for this book, the longtime facilitator Mark Jones described his understanding of the role that emotional vulnerability plays in his work: "If I understand the process of my own suffering and pain, my own rage and despair, my own sense of irrelevance or nonconnectedness, that gives me insights into how other people are feeling. And that shared experience enables me to go from nothing to sympathy to empathy and compassion."[3] As Mark suggests, when we allow ourselves to awaken to our own suffering, we connect ourselves to the larger world of pain and to the people we are here to serve.

Emotional openness means opening our hearts to difficult as well as pleasurable emotions and feeling them fully—observing and experiencing them—without allowing those emotions to carry us away. When we can open our heart up to joy, hope, and passion, we are more able to stoke the creative energy of group fire. When we allow our heart to feel pain, suffering, and despair, we unleash the cleansing and restorative potential of group fire. When we can feel the wide range of emotions without melting into fight or flight, gently cradling our own heart, we become a cradle for the heart of everyone in the room.

SELF-ACCEPTANCE

We reject in others those parts that we most reject in ourselves. This is never more true than when we are standing in the fire, watching the drama of people who are struggling with conflict and complexity and feeling uncertain that their efforts will be successful. If vulnerability teaches us to experience and name our own strong emotions, self-acceptance enables us to embrace the source of our emotions. Self-acceptance involves claiming and befriending the parts of ourselves about which we feel ashamed, embarrassed, and fearful.

Working in groups is perhaps the best way to discover those parts of ourselves that we would prefer to keep in the shadows. David Sibbett, a facilitator and thought leader, reflected on his own journey toward self-acceptance during his interview for this book: "If someone is totally annoying me, I've come to believe that annoyance is a function of my own non-self-acceptance."[4] Every label we assign, every judgment we make, every feeling we have, is an opportunity to look inside and ask, *What part of me am I projecting in this moment? What part of me needs to be identified and accepted?*

It took me many years to realize that my harsh judgments of others were really expressions of my self-hate. For a long time, I would become impatient and angry with group participants who were not speaking up. I would judge them as cowardly, thinking, "We have created this wonderful space for them to share their viewpoints, and they are literally making themselves invisible. That's not only cowardly but also stupid. They are squandering this opportunity." In those moments, I was resenting the part of myself that was less assertive and less comfortable speaking my mind in the presence of power and opposition.

When we learn to accept the whole package of who we are and make allies of our shadows, we are less susceptible to impulsively judging, idealizing, stereotyping, and rejecting the people around us. When we embrace those qualities about which we have felt uncomfortable or ashamed, we are less likely to become anxious, irritated, suspicious, or arrogant with others.

Self-acceptance is the work of a lifetime. Unless we can learn to become honest and kind to ourselves, we will always encounter the limitations of our projections. Mark Hodge, a facilitator who works in India, shared, "I can now recognize the wounds in my life that I need to heal, and as a result I have a greater appreciation of these kinds of wounds in others." The majority of the veteran facilitators I interviewed have taken this work of self-acceptance very seriously, recognizing it as a path not only to professional excellence but also to personal fulfillment. They have cultivated this capacity in many ways,

including psychotherapy, mindfulness meditation, and participation in T-groups. Whatever
the path, the goal remains consistent—to know
and embrace all parts of ourselves.

AWARENESS OF
THE WHOLE PERSON

We quickly decide who people are. We take in a few bits of data—
clothes, tone of voice, title, ethnicity, public reputation, mastery of language, and a few behaviors. We combine these observations with our
own experiences and biases, and our brains create a label—we decide
we know who a person is. He is an expert. She is a real leader. He
has a political agenda. She is manipulative. He is the decisive CEO.
She is just the dock supervisor. We act as if people exist solely in the
context of the meeting, the organization, or a particular issue. We too
quickly forget that every person who walks into the room has a larger
life story.

We can never know another person completely. Much of our work as
facilitators involves collaborating with stakeholders in a structured setting for a set period of time. Seeing the whole person doesn't mean learning
the life story and motivations of every participant with whom we work.
Instead, it involves an ongoing awareness that each person we encounter
is much more than the person who is showing up in that moment, in that
meeting, on that day. We strengthen our capacity for compassion when
we can hold this question as a mantra: *Who else is this person?*

Asking myself this question opens my heart to the possibility that the
"angry" 55-year-old CEO who is looking in my direction with crossed
arms, squinting eyes, and a frown may also be a son to an aging mother,
an aspiring painter, a daddy who reads each night to his children; he
may be anxious about how he is perceived by others, deep in thought,

distracted by his sister's terminal illness, wanting to make a connection with me, struggling with a new pair of contact lenses, or trying desperately to digest the breakfast burrito he shouldn't have eaten before the meeting. Perhaps he is all those things and more. Asking the question opens my heart and enables me to avoid reacting to my narrow "angry CEO" story as if it's the only story.

UNCONDITIONAL POSITIVE REGARD

Even in the midst of their most reactive moments, we must find it within ourselves to recognize the worth of others. We must learn to see those who are acting from anger as being worthy of respect and honor. This way of seeing others extends dignity to them. My friend and colleague Ruben Perczek has taught me a lot about the meaning of dignity. He said to me, "In receiving and honoring the worth in myself, I open space to receive others, extending dignity to them. Dignity isn't so much about what one is doing or saying. It's a way of being that conveys that no one is to be taken for granted."[5]

The term *unconditional positive regard* originated with psychotherapy pioneer Carl Rogers. It refers to an unwavering support and acceptance of people as worthy of our respect, regardless of what they are doing in the moment. Extending this kind of positive regard means approaching difficult behaviors without ridicule or criticism. This doesn't mean that we have to agree with or condone everything that people do. We hold on to our guiding intention and integrity. However, our interventions are free from condescension and derision.

I have had to reflect a lot on what it means to extend dignity while at the same time confronting behavior that is having a negative impact on the group. For example, even as I find myself intervening for the eighth time to point out to a client that he is once again interrupting a team member, I maintain a deep sense of liking him and a real appreciation for his personal struggle with impulsiveness. Positive regard often challenges us to actively search the heart for reasons to respect people in their worst moments. When I find my heart closing and patience and compassion fading away, I often say one of these statements to myself in order to reconnect with my regard for the person:

> *I respect you as the unique individual I am coming to know.*
> *I respect that you have a different way of looking at things.*
> *I respect that you react differently than I might want you to.*
> *I respect that you came here to do this difficult work.*
> *I respect that this is a moment in which it's normal to struggle.*

Positive regard sets up a wholehearted alliance between us and group members—one in which they feel safe and confident about expressing their truths.

What Shifts When We Stand with Compassion?

When we learn to feel our own suffering, identify our projections, and see others as whole and worthy human beings regardless of their behavior in the moment, our presence brings *healing*, *trust*, and *love* into the fire.

HEALING

People often come to the meetings we lead feeling alienated, wounded, and fearful. And they know that every moment in the fire holds the risk of more wounds. So when they experience compassion, gentleness, and acceptance from us, they begin to feel whole again. When they can safely express their fears, joy, hopes, and suffering, they remember what it means to be connected to their own hearts and to the hearts of others. As our stance of compassion enables healing to occur in the group, the possibilities also expand for shared understanding, forgiveness, and collective action.

TRUST

There is no more essential element to the work of collaboration than trust. As conveners, we carry special authority. For better or for worse, people look to us to help them establish a safe container for high-stakes conversations. If we embrace the wide variety of personalities and hold them all worthy of our respect, people trust that they can be authentic. They trust that they can bring their truth to the table. They sense that if they violate a principle or agreement, we will approach them with warmth and understanding. When they see us acting with trust and compassion toward their adversaries, their hearts are given permission to open toward one another.

LOVE

Our meetings are microcosms of our organizations and communities. Every time we come together in conversation, we hope to become more than we have been in the past—more productive, more collaborative, and yes, more loving. In a room filled with closed hearts, one compassionate heart is enough. Our greatest leaders have understood that their transformational abilities came not from their words but from their willingness to show vulnerability and to extend dignity. The love that is created through standing with compassion is more than a feeling. It is a resonant organizing energy—the kind of fire that brings once-dormant seeds to life.

TO STAND WITH COMPASSION MEANS REMEMBERING
that we *all* struggle with uncertainty, contradictions, and
pain as we search for collective wisdom and common
ground. It means that even when people are not living up
to our expectations, we acknowledge their struggle and
suffering. Compassion is neither pity nor sympathy. In fact,
it sometimes requires that we confront others. Our capacity to embody patience and gentleness in the face of people
and behaviors that we might judge as inappropriate, hurtful, or evil is the most powerful way we can stand as fire
tenders. And it is often the most challenging.

QUESTIONS FOR REFLECTION

- What enables you to maintain an open, compassionate
  heart in the presence of others who are acting in ways you
  find to be distasteful or who are undermining the goals of
  the meeting?

- When have you allowed yourself to be emotionally open?
  What do you still not allow yourself to feel fully?

- What do people do that hooks you in meetings? What
  qualities and behaviors do you find difficult to accept in
  others? In what ways might they be connected to qualities
  within yourself that you have not yet accepted?

- Who in your life currently gives you unconditional positive
  regard? What do you feel when you are with them?

The Deep Democracy practitioner Myrna Lewis suggested this activity.[6] Think of the last meeting participant who really annoyed you in some way. This is a person in whose presence you felt a shortage of neutrality and compassion. Now pair up with a partner and play the role of this person. Really exaggerate the person's words, tone, facial expressions, and physical gestures. Even if you become uncomfortable with the level of exaggeration, continue the role-play. If you carry on being this person, you will discover a part of yourself that this person represents. Take time to debrief with your partner and reflect on the aspects of this person with which you identify.

PRACTICES

In the preceding chapters we looked at the importance of our interior states when we're helping groups navigate through uncertainty and strong emotions. The six ways of standing cannot simply be summoned when they are needed. The capacities associated with each way of standing must be continuously culti-vated and strengthened as psychological, spiritual, emotional, and physical "muscle memory."

Inner-directed practices keep us on the journey of self-discovery and self-mastery. These practices foster awareness and create readiness. Practices help us to make friends with our emotional hot buttons; to move beyond our habitual ways of seeing, thinking, and doing; and to overcome the seduction of ego. They acquaint us with our strengths, affirm our purpose, and keep us connected to our inner wisdom. Through practices, we gain confidence that we can embody a way of being in which we have the greatest capacity for clear seeing and effective action.

Just because we know something doesn't mean we can always embody it. Practice allows us to gain experience working with our thoughts, emotions, and physical states in a variety of contexts so that over time we become better able to embody the six ways of standing. For example, I know about the importance of suspending judgments when I am trying to remain impartial and receptive to other points of view. Despite this knowledge, an arrogant, skeptical, stubborn side of me has a way of occasionally showing up uninvited.

Personal practices during "cooler" times help us to form a familiar, accessible center from which to keep our balance in the midst of human firestorms. They also provide the means by which we are able to recover after losing our footing. Practices offer the space to make mistakes and to harvest the lessons that our missteps create. Our practices can take the form of physical or mental activity. They can be sole endeavors or grounded in social interaction. Practices can have a creative, even improvisational nature to them, or they can be highly ritualistic. Personal practices have most potency and integrity when they are done with (1) a clear motivation, (2) a high level of consistency, (3) mindfulness about what we are learning, and (4) gentleness toward the self so that when clarity and consistency falter, we are able to move back into practice without self-aggression or resistance.

While consistent mindful practices expand our knowledge and skillfulness as conveners, their more essential purpose is to shape who we are being as we navigate through complex deliberations, conflicts, and process breakdowns. Practices enable us to create a set of new and more useful "default" ways of being in the fire, which over time can replace responses driven by impulsiveness, self-protection, and emotion.

The developmental practices that any one of us chooses can originate in many places. While I strongly advocate that every leader have a set of inner-directed practices, I do not attempt to prescribe a standard set. Many in-depth books have been written about such practices, some of which are listed at the conclusion of this book. The following chapters offer some broad categories and specific examples in the hope that you will be inspired to design and sustain your own unique portfolio of supportive practices.

■

CULTIVATE EVERYDAY READINESS

I'm a strong believer in the importance of my ongoing practices for helping me be present, unattached, and calm in the face of whatever messiness shows up in the room.

—Peggy Holman

Process Consultant and Author,

The Change Handbook

GREAT DANCERS AND MUSICIANS invest thousands of hours practicing their craft before the curtain goes up. In order to ensure excellence during a game, athletes practice mental focus and technical skills well before they walk onto the playing field or court. Likewise, fire tenders must have an ongoing set of practices that prepare us to be at our best as leaders.

This chapter describes the value of ongoing inner-directed practices that assist us in achieving a relaxed and focused state of being, unburden us from limiting beliefs and stories, help us access our compassion, and remind us of our purpose and gifts. We will also examine the special challenges of starting and sustaining everyday practices as well as the benefits of such practices for preparing us to work in high-heat situations.

Why Ongoing Practices?

The best way to be ready for incendiary moments in groups is to develop solid habits of mind, heart, and body under less intense conditions. Through practices that we cultivate every day, we become intimately acquainted with our unique vulnerabilities, identify our limiting patterns of thought and behavior, and find methods that enable us to move into the calm and deliberate state through which our best leadership can be expressed. Ongoing practices enable us to create new default responses that over time replace our very human but less helpful defensive reactions.

Ongoing practices are used outside the context of high-heat meetings, but as you will see in the following chapters, they can also be drawn on in the midst of challenging meetings. Many of us have daily, weekly, and even yearly practices. The time invested in each may range from three minutes to three days, depending on the particular practice. Though the duration is less important than the intention and quality of practice, there is no denying that thirty minutes of focused practice will yield more for you than fifteen minutes of the same-quality practice.

Ongoing practices set the stage and establish the discipline for many of the other practices covered in subsequent chapters. If you want to master in-the-moment recovery from being triggered, you must have an ongoing "centering" practice in your life. If you need to learn to access compassion when others are acting in ways that you find to be distasteful, you are not likely to be able to shift beyond resentment or annoyance in the moment unless you have an ongoing heart-opening routine you practice outside meetings.

Once an ongoing practice becomes an integral part of your life, it feels less like a commitment or burden and more like brushing your teeth—something you do naturally and without which you would not feel quite right. When an ongoing inner-directed practice like centering or self-inquiry becomes embedded in your routine, the benefits are significant. You are more aware of yourself and others, and you use that awareness to make more deliberate choices. You have an expanded range of choices from which to draw because you have cultivated new ways of standing that are aligned with your guiding intention.

Ongoing practices enable us to create new default responses that over time replace our very human but less helpful defensive reactions.

Ongoing inner-directed practices enable us to quickly recognize and free ourselves from habitual ways of interpreting situations. They heighten our awareness of our physical and emotional states and teach us how to shift into the kind of relaxed and centered state from which wise choices can be made.

What Kinds of Ongoing Practices Make Sense?

I suggest ongoing practices that strengthen mental, emotional, and physical self-awareness; help us to examine and shed limiting internal narratives that disable us in the fire; build new habits for inducing relaxation, clarity, and compassion; and provide opportunities to experiment with standing in the face of high-heat situations.

How you design a combination of practices is a very personal enterprise. If you are just getting started, I recommend that you select a single ongoing practice—one that you feel motivated to practice regularly. In selecting practices to pursue, ask yourself the following questions:

- Which of the interior capacities from part II would I like to cultivate in my work and life?

- How much time am I willing to invest each week in a consistent mindful practice?

- Is there a practice or a combination of practices that will attend to all four dimensions of my development as a fire tender—mental, emotional, physical, and spiritual?

- What is my motive beyond any short-term result? Why does any chosen practice make sense for my work and my life?

As you think about these questions, be aware of the tendency to want to do it all. Be realistic and start with one ongoing practice that you can build on. If you do not already have an ongoing practice for centering, begin here.

Bring a Relaxed Attention to the Moment

Fire tending involves standing in the face of emotional intensity and uncertainty. In these moments our minds often go on autopilot, fill with impulsive chatter, and drown out the internal voice of wisdom. Our hot buttons will inevitably be pushed, and the average person risks responding in a less-than-effective reactive manner. What sets fire tenders apart is that we are capable of going into very challenging meetings with clarity, calm, and focus; we can maintain that state while in the midst of strong emotions; and we can recover quickly when we get triggered.

This state of relaxed focus is the starting point for heightened self-awareness and deliberate action: standing in the here and now. From this state we can mobilize our resourcefulness for coping, adapting, and bouncing back.

A wide variety of practices are aimed at achieving a mindful, calm, focused state. They include contemplative practices like deep relaxation, conscious breathing, yoga, prayer, and tai chi. Two practices that are particularly powerful in moving us into a state of peacefulness and heightened awareness are *physical centering* and *mindfulness meditation*.

PHYSICAL CENTERING

The purpose of centering is to bring awareness and relaxation to the body in ways that beneficially affect our mental and emotional state. The master somatic coach Victoria Castle taught me a simple two-step approach for physical centering.[1] Try this while you are standing.

1. **Attend.** Notice your physical sensations. What do you notice about the depth of your breathing, your heart rate, and your muscle tension? What are you conscious about regarding your posture, the distribution of your weight, and your facial expression in this moment? Scan your body for whatever you can observe.

2. **Adjust.** Inhale and exhale slowly and deeply so that your stomach expands with each breadth. Relax your muscles, letting your weight rest on your hips, legs, and feet instead of holding it in your neck and shoulders. Let your facial muscles, particularly your jaw muscles, relax. Once your entire body is relaxed, assume a taller, wider stance, allowing your head to extend upward and your feet to spread to shoulder width. Feel your feet on the floor and notice the vertical and horizontal space you occupy.

At first, this centering practice may take several minutes to complete. With experience you will be able to center yourself in a few seconds. The more we stay centered, the more alert we are to the present moment and therefore the more adaptable we are to whatever is happening in the room. When we are centered, we are ready to shift into whatever way of standing will serve our purpose and effectiveness in the fire. As we will see in chapter 11, the centered state is the jumping-off point for wise action.

MINDFULNESS MEDITATION

Broadly speaking, meditation is a path by which we are led from within toward a greater state of calm, self-awareness, and focus. For facilitators of high-heat meetings, meditation teaches us to get comfortable with restlessness, excitement, worry, judgment, and other disruptive inventions of the mind. Mindfulness meditation teaches us to observe our thoughts and feelings without judgment and then to return to our focus on the breath. In high-heat situations, this can be an invaluable practice for avoiding being swept up in the emotion and intensity of the group.

In a mindful state, we are able to regard our thoughts as something to be observed and not necessarily acted on. We are alert and draw on our highest intelligence. This practice does not involve going into a trance or actively suppressing feelings and thoughts. To the contrary, when we are engaged in mindfulness meditation, we are aware moment to moment of our thoughts and feelings as passing phenomena that neither preoccupy nor define us. Here are some basic steps for initiating an everyday mindfulness meditation practice.

1. Find a quiet and comfortable place to sit in a chair or on the floor. Find a place where you can feel connected to the earth. If you are just getting started with this practice, it's useful to set a timer. Give yourself permission to begin with periods of two or three minutes, gradually increasing the time of your sitting.

2. Sit with your head, neck, and back straight but not stiff. Try doing this practice with your eyes open, but allow your vision to become soft and diffused.

3. Do your best to set aside thoughts of the past and future and focus your mind on the here and now of your breathing.

4. Focus on the sensation of air moving in and out of your body as you breathe. Experience the rise and fall of your belly and the sensation of air entering and leaving your nostrils. Notice the quality of each breath.

5. Watch every thought come and go, whether it is a grocery list, something you forgot to do, a past conversation, or a preoccupation about what might happen next. When any kind of thought comes into your mind, don't ignore or suppress it. Rather, make note of it, remain calm, and use your breathing as an anchor.

6. If you notice yourself becoming involved in your thoughts, observe where your mind went, without judging, and return to your breathing. Remember to be gentle with yourself when this happens.

7. As the time comes to a close, sit for a minute or two, becoming aware of where you are. Get up gradually.

Mindfulness meditation teaches us the invaluable habit of letting go of thoughts and feelings that tend to weaken our integrity and undermine our ability to act wisely when the downward spiral of a group's energy is strong. So, when faced with a challenging group dynamic that may threaten our sense of control or competency, we aren't pulled off center and into a reactive mode. Instead, we learn to name our regrets, worries, predictions, and judgments as "thoughts" that fade into the background as we return to the present moment.

Both centering and mindfulness meditation are core practices for fire tenders. They enhance our ability to recognize and slow down patterns of emotional reactivity—to stand with self-awareness. They increase our comfort with stillness and non-action—to stand calmly in the here and now, often a powerful intervention in itself. Both practices reduce stress by providing an ever-available focal point—our breathing—as a tool for remaining relaxed and in the present moment.

Transform Limiting Thoughts and Feelings

We've examined the instinctive and learned habits that often undermine our effectiveness in moments of high heat. A variety of inner-directed practices when consistently used enable us to quickly recognize and free ourselves from negative habitual ways of thinking, seeing, feeling, and acting. Since we can change only what we can see, we need practices that bring hidden assumptions, unconscious interpretations, and emotional hot buttons into clear view.

One way to become more familiar with our limiting patterns is to take systematic stock of our self-generated "stories" and to question their validity. *Self-inquiry* practices are based on the assumption that humans need less advice and more space to access what Parker Palmer calls "the inner teacher, a voice of truth, that offers the guidance and power we need to deal with our problems."[2] Inquiry practices pose a set of questions that enable us to hold our beliefs up to the light and learn more about them. They are not intended to embarrass us into changing. Rather, they are grounded in candor, curiosity, and supportiveness. When this kind of inquiry is practiced in calmer moments over many years, it can be a very powerful discipline, yielding immediate insights and perspective when we are feeling the heat of an intense interaction.

Through self-inquiry practices we can explore a set of questions about our beliefs, assumptions, emotional patterns, habitual ways of reacting, and ways in which we view ourselves. In self-inquiry we also can explore our strengths, sources of inner wisdom, convictions, and purpose. Among the inquiry practices that colleagues and I have found to be most helpful are *self-guided inquiry*, *peer mentor relationships*, and *clearness committees*.

SELF-GUIDED INQUIRY

Many books offer self-guided approaches to inquiry, including *Loving What Is* by Byron Katie, *Change Your Questions, Change Your Life* by Marilee Adams, and *Feeding Your Demons* by Tsultrim Allione. While the approaches of these books are quite different, all offer self-guided, question-based processes designed to deepen our insight into the interior self as well as transform the ways we see and act on our exterior world. You will enhance the value of your self-guided inquiry process if you:

- Schedule time each day to reflect on an issue or question

- Pick a time and physical space free from interruption or distraction

- Choose physical surroundings that relax and inspire you

- Keep a journal of experiences, insights, and important shifts in your thinking

- Review your journal every few weeks to notice any emerging patterns

My ongoing practice of self-inquiry is to notice when I am getting stuck, frustrated, or pulled down and to ask myself these questions: *What's the story I am running with right now? What is the belief that this story justifies or relies on? How is that belief serving me in this moment? What other beliefs might I adopt that better serve my intention and integrity in this moment?* Other self-inquiry questions were offered in chapter 3 in the section on reflective processing.

I was reminded of the value of self-inquiry practice when I was hired to facilitate a board retreat for a not-for-profit organization called 1% for the Planet. The organization was started by Patagonia founder Yvon Chouinard, who has been a hero of mine for decades because of his visionary leadership in creating a successful company committed to environmental sustainability. As we sat together over dinner that night, I noticed my preoccupation with any signals as to whether Yvon liked me. I wanted desperately to impress him, and it was resulting in an uncharacteristic nervous chattiness. After dinner I went up to my room and reflected on my internal story that Yvon's approval of me mattered. My story was that he was more important and wiser than the other board members. I realized that if I carried this belief into the next day's board meeting, it would undermine my ability to be decisive and impartial. It came to me in that moment that I could be at my best only if I embraced an alternative belief—that Yvon was one of many important leaders in the room and that his approval or disapproval of me was mostly up to him, not me. I walked into the meeting the next day with a stronger sense of authenticity, focus, and impartiality, having relieved myself of the need to impress the legendary CEO.

Interestingly, at the end of the retreat he expressed to another participant how great it was to be in a board meeting where he genuinely felt like one of many voices rather than the celebrity to whom people deferred. Because self-inquiry is an ongoing practice for me, it was available in a moment when I was feeling nervous and inauthentic.

An alternative to the solo approach is to find a neutral individual to facilitate your inquiry. A neutral party can probe for deeper insights, reflect your observations back to you, and point out inconsistencies that may suggest rationalizations or blind spots. A partner can be a qualified psychotherapist or a counselor, coach, or mentor. When partnering with someone, it is important to realize that you are a responsible member of the inquiry and not a passive recipient of questions. You should be actively involved in identifying the topics and framing the questions for the inquiry.

PEER MENTOR RELATIONSHIPS

A peer mentor is a trusted colleague with whom you meet on a regular schedule, say every four to six weeks. If your goal is to work specifically on building your self-awareness of mental habits, emotional hot buttons, and ego, then that should be the agreed-upon focus of the inquiry. Among the questions you might ask each other are:

- When do you typically feel overwhelmed, insecure, resistant, or resentful in the meetings you facilitate?

- What beliefs or assumptions are operating when you experience these states?

- How true are these beliefs?

- In what ways do these beliefs support or undermine your ability to be in service to the group and to lead with integrity?

- What beliefs about yourself in your work tend to get you into trouble?

CLEARNESS COMMITTEES

Clearness committees originated as a Quaker practice more than three hundred years ago and have been popularized by Parker Palmer and the Center for Courage and Renewal. Clearness committees involve a "focus person" bringing an issue to a selected group of five or six trusted people. After a moment of centering silence, the focus person describes the issue with which they are struggling and provides the relevant background and thoughts about what lies ahead. Those sitting in the circle are forbidden from speaking to the focus person in any way except to ask an honest, open question aimed at helping the focus person deepen his or her understanding of the problem. No advice, reassurances, or problem fixing is permitted—just questions and silent reflection. The ambience of a clearness committee is slow, spacious, gentle, and relaxed.

The central assumption of clearness committees is that we all have what Parker Palmer calls an "inner teacher" or a "deeper knowing" about our challenges, gifts, questions, and callings. The organizational development consultant Diane Robbins described how both the practice and underlying principles of the clearness committee have served as a source of profound growth: "When we have a clearness committee guided by these careful principles and practices, we create a powerful holding environment unlike any I have ever witnessed. The practice of open and honest questions in this setting has repeatedly proven to me that our inner teacher is alive and well when it is invited into speech in a safe space."[3]

Self-directed inquiry practices help us cultivate our ability to move beyond limiting patterns of seeing and thinking. As self-inquiry practices become a routine part of our lives, we realize that they can be applied to any of the six ways of standing and more specifically to the different capacities described in part II. For example, we might explore the beliefs and assumptions that undermine or strengthen our ability to be compassionate. We might explore our attachments that get in the way of flexibility and high-integrity action in the fire. Or we might discover the patterns of beliefs and judgments we hold that undermine our ability to maintain an open mind.

Access Compassion

At its core, leadership is a human endeavor. The ability to open our hearts is a key leverage point for many other ways of standing, including dancing with surprises and standing with an open mind. Every minute of every day, we are presented with opportunities to extend authentic compassion toward other humans as well as toward ourselves.

Compassion practices enable us to see the ways in which suffering and pain manifest themselves in the world. These practices encourage us to take down our interior walls of self-protection in order to witness and feel the vast array of emotions that make us human. Compassion practices offer us ways to experience our connectedness with all living beings and to cultivate gratitude for the small and large gifts that come in unexpected, sometimes unattractive wrapping.

Two simple ways to cultivate compassion on a daily basis are the practices of *compassion journaling* and *compassion breathing*.

COMPASSION JOURNALING

A compassion journal is a log of experiences that evoke emotions—both pleasant and unpleasant. We can capture moments that give us great joy and satisfaction. We can record the qualities and deeds of others for which we are grateful. We might make note of the driver who came to a full stop and smiled as we passed through the crosswalk. In addition to the sources of satisfaction, joy, and gratitude, a compassion journal should include the moments of suffering and pain we witness during the course of our day and the instances in which we are aggressive toward or unforgiving of ourselves. As this becomes an ongoing practice, we develop a heightened awareness of our emotional state and that of others. Our hearts become more tuned in to what is happening around us.

COMPASSION BREATHING

Compassion breathing is another practice designed to open our hearts. Several years ago I learned about this process from two sources—the environmental activists Joanna Macy and Molly Young Brown, and the Buddhist teacher Pema Chödrön. Known as *tonglen* to Buddhist practitioners, its purpose is to strengthen our capacity to stand in the face of suffering while maintaining a compassionate and resilient heart. Chödrön describes it as a way to "use difficult situations—poisons—as fuel for waking up."[4] Every day there are opportunities to practice breathing through the suffering, grief, and pain we encounter. We encounter it on the street. We watch it on the news. We experience it in our homes and within our own hearts. Tonglen is an antidote for the self-numbing and isolation we engage in as a response to our fear of suffering.

The practice of compassion breathing involves identifying anything that feels distasteful, painful, or distressing. Instead of attempting to repress or deny it, we breathe it in and connect with it fully. As we breathe in the suffering and grief—our own and that of others—we let the heaviness of the in-breath pass through the nose, throat, lungs, and heart, not holding on to it but letting it flow through the body. We breathe in the suffering not only as our own specific experience but also as part of the larger human condition. In doing so, we feel a kinship with the larger web of life. On the out-breath we send out a wish for happiness, relaxation, or whatever will relieve the suffering that we breathed in. As we exhale, we do so with a sense of openness and relief.

Practices that increase compassion enhance our ability to stand in the face of challenging human behavior, suffering, and pain without judgment, distraction, or resentment. As we develop comfort with the many facets of our own emotional landscape, we become more accepting of the diversity of human emotions that show up when people gather to work on complex and high-stakes issues. Having an ongoing and consistent compassion-strengthening practice helps us cultivate a capacity for emotional openness, self-acceptance, awareness of the whole person, and unconditional regard. In addition, we become less attached to "fixing" difficult emotions as we learn to appreciate the value of witnessing—stillness, suspension of judgment, and letting go—in the face of suffering.

Affirm Our Purpose, Remember Our Gifts

In the swirl and intensity of group conflict and confusion, I can sometimes barely remember my name, let alone what I have to offer the group. In those moments I am susceptible to making poor choices or acting on impulse. A regular practice affirming who I am in my work has been very important in helping to reinforce what we called *knowing what you stand for*. It also helps me define the internal gyroscope I call guiding intention.

An affirmation is an authentic, heartfelt declaration of what you want to contribute in the world, the gifts you offer, or the future you want to bring into being. Peggy Holman, a convener of Open Space meetings, has had a daily affirmation practice since 1986. She chooses one or two affirmations to work on for a period of one year. Over the years, her affirmations have evolved into questions. "Right now I am holding a personal question and a collective question that I speak daily, usually in the shower," she says. "How am I a spark to grow love's capacity in myself, in others, and in the whole? How do we seed, grow, and evolve enlightened organizations and inspired communities?"[5]

What would you like to remind yourself of each day? Several years ago I sat down and wrote an affirmation for myself. I carry it with me, and though I do not recite it on a daily basis, it is a regular part of my ongoing mindfulness practice whenever I step into a meeting room. Here's what it says:

> I am a light for the wisdom that needs illuminating.
> I am a cradle for the hearts that need safe haven.
> I am a drum for all the voices that want to be heard.
> I am a trowel making space for the seeds of possibility.

An affirmation is more powerful if it is personal. You can write your own affirmation by following these steps:

1. Take some time to write three to four sentences answering these questions:
   - What qualities, gifts, motives, and callings do you want to be reminded of each day?
   - What are you here to contribute in the world?
   - Think about the person in your life who is your most avid supporter and cheerleader. In your moment of greatest self-doubt, what would you want this person to whisper in your ear?

2. Now, craft these ideas into a three- to four-line affirmation— a statement that will fit on a piece of paper as big as a business card. Print out a pocket-size version to keep with you.

3. Commit to thirty days of reciting it *out loud* every day until you know it like you know your own name.

Practice in the Heat

Many of the ongoing practices described thus far can be carried out in the context of a relatively safe and comfortable environment. As these practices form new, positive habits in our work, we want to look for

incremental ways to expose ourselves to high-
heat situations. It's impossible to develop a
mastery of standing in the fire without spending time in the fire. In fact, some psychologists
believe that the only real way people become
skilled at dealing with relationship hot spots
and flare-ups is by engaging these capacities
when they are feeling most triggered.

Pay attention to
encounters with
friends and family
members who ex-
press opinions you
might label "stupid,"
"outdated," even
"bigoted."

BE A MEETING PARTICIPANT

The process consultant Chris Grant suggests that we all make a point of
regularly participating in meetings as non-facilitator, non-leader members—as just part of the gang. This practice heightens our sensitivity to
what it means to participate in a group process. As group members, we
gain empathy and appreciation for what it is like to attempt to influence others, struggle with differences, and conform to a process someone else designed.

STEP INTO YOUR ALLERGY ZONE

Another heat-exposing practice is one I call stepping into your allergy
zone. It involves seeking out ideas and people we might otherwise
avoid. These are ideas and people we tend to experience as uncomfortable, distasteful, and even offensive. Attend public talks by people
who hold viewpoints opposed to yours. Listen to radio programs with
commentators who make you want to scream when you are alone in
your car. Pay attention to encounters with friends and family members who express opinions you might label "stupid," "outdated," even
"bigoted." In all these cases, take time to inquire sincerely and openly
into their beliefs and assumptions. Notice your internal judgments and
reactions. How open are you to what is being said? What is your level

of curiosity? What are the ways in which you can acknowledge a very different viewpoint without having to agree with it?

PARTNER WITH A CO-FACILITATOR

Interestingly, one of the best ways to create heat for oneself is to partner with a co-facilitator. Co-facilitating requires a high degree of trust, openness, flexibility, compromise, and the ability to keep one's ego in check. Like marriage, working partnerships are wonderful opportunities to learn about our personal hot buttons and gifts. Co-facilitating provides continuous tests as to how we deal with conflict, criticism, and the need for control. Co-facilitators see us when we are confused and anxious. They come to know our triggers and blind spots, sometimes better than we know them ourselves. They appreciate our strengths and are there to back us up in our moments of weakness. They sometimes drive us crazy with their idiosyncrasies, imperfections, and insecurities, but we can't help but learn from their insight and skill.

FACILITATE MEETINGS

Finally, at the risk of being obvious, facilitate meetings—any meetings. To one degree or another, fire exists in every meeting. Even where there is no visible conflict or confusion, there is heat. When people veer off topic, what is the fire you create within yourself? As time is ticking away and a long-winded participant doesn't appear to be running out of new ways to say the same thing, what hot button gets pushed? As people project their fantasies onto your leadership as the reason the meeting will succeed, do you get hooked by that expectation? Notice when you feel anxiety, self-righteousness, or boredom. As you facilitate, play with your own attitudinal, emotional, and physical ways of standing. Fire takes many forms. Every meeting is an opportunity to experiment with the different ways of standing in it.

Making Everyday Readiness Practices Work

I am someone who has difficulty with consistency and perseverance when it comes to practice. I have a low tolerance for routine and discomfort. And in a sense, my struggle with regular, intentional practice has become the most important aspect of my personal practice. Many of the same things that trip me up in practice and in my ongoing interior development trip me up in the fire of meetings—unrealistic expectations of myself, self-doubt, a desire for immediate gratification, a need for control, and self-blame when things are not going as planned. I have come to learn as much about myself during the lapses in my practice as I have in the practices themselves.

If you say to yourself, "I already know how to stand well without having to build a whole regimen of practices into my life," ask yourself whose voice that is. It may be the voice of accurate self-assessment, but it may be the voice of resistance to change, or the voice of fear. Learning to distinguish among the many internal voices—those that support and those that undermine growth—is all part of making practice work.

As you think about initiating and sustaining a set of ongoing practices that support your journey of self-mastery, here are some thoughts from someone who is still figuring out how to make this work.

First, you will face two primary challenges: busyness and boredom. Our lives are overloaded with obligations, activities, and stimulation. Our calendars are cluttered, and we often believe that everything on our plate is a top priority. Though this level of busyness isn't sustainable physically or mentally, we can't imagine taking time to sit still and just be.

Boredom stems from the cultural expectation that everything must be entertaining or productive. Gratification and productivity drive much of how we choose to spend our time. Many of the practices are inner directed and not intended to entertain or to produce anything tangible. These two challenges will not go away, but their influence can be minimized. Here are some guidelines for building practices for everyday readiness into your life:

Start realistically. Select a single practice like centering, and work with it for a period of time on terms that you know you can manage. Schedule the practice on your calendar if you need to guard the time, and make sure that you are scheduling it at a time when you can devote undivided attention to it. Generally speaking, there is no "right" time except the time you can give your full self to the practice.

Appreciate yourself. The purpose of practice is not to repair your flaws. Bring to your practice the fundamental assumption that you possess gifts, strengths, and the best of intentions. Harvey Schechter, my very first boss in my very first job out of college, used to lean back in his chair and say to me, "Larry, you did this perfectly. Now let me show you how to do it better." Harvey's humorous words are a reminder that we are complete just as we are—and for those of us on the path of mastery, there is always room to be even better.

Let go of expectations about how quickly and smoothly the learning will go. Some of these practices seem simple when you read about them and are quite challenging when you do them. You will learn a lot by simply noticing the kinds of expectations—"shoulds"—you lay onto your practice. Notice your expectations and then let them dissolve away. Practice is not about outcomes but about doing the practice.

Make an honest commitment to engage in the practice regardless of how stressed, distracted, tired, or busy you are on any given day. You may make all kinds of rationalizations and excuses for not practicing, but you should know that the times you find it least convenient to engage in your ongoing practices are the times you will benefit the most. And when you do go for a while without practicing, return to it without self-abuse or guilt. Simply resume.

Build systems of support. Find partners or communities in which you can enjoy, refine, and deepen your practice. Develop pre- and post-practice rituals that set the stage and that reinforce your commitment. These might include lighting a candle, making a cup of tea, preparing a special place, playing enjoyable music, wearing certain clothing, or reading a passage from an inspiring book prior to or after your practice.

PRACTICES FOR CULTIVATING EVERYDAY READINESS are ongoing inner-directed practices we build into our lives. They teach us new and productive habits so that we don't need to think too hard when we must shift from a reactive state to a relaxed and centered one. Through ongoing practices we develop our mental, emotional, and physical awareness. These practices help us examine internal narratives that disable us in the fire. They help us nurture new habits for inducing relaxation, clarity, strength, and compassion when others are anxious and angry. Through everyday practice we shape our way of being in ways that, over time, close the gap between our choices and our guiding intention.

■ What is the role of "practice" in your life? What practices do you do with intention and consistency, and how do they contribute to your health, effectiveness, and happiness?

■ Which of your current ongoing practices prepare and support you in your work with high-stakes, high-heat groups? What purpose is served by each of these practices?

■ What new ongoing practices are you considering? What benefits do you hope to gain from each of these practices?

PREPARE
TO LEAD

If I'm to work successfully with others, I have to

remember who I am. So before "we" show up,

I do a bit of "me work" and remember who I am.

—Chris Grant

Process Facilitator, 14A Conversations

FOR MANY LEADERS AND FACILITATORS, what happens just before the meeting is largely a matter of agenda review, materials production, and logistics related to the meeting space. Those are important activities. However, there are other important practices related to preparing. These enable us to settle into our own rhythm and intention for the day, connect with meeting participants on a human level, sense the mood in the room, and do the little things that help to create a container in which people will be able to do their best work together.

Many world-class athletes and musicians engage in extensive rituals just before entering the playing field or stage. While some of their practices are driven by superstition, many serve the much deeper function of centering, focusing, and moving into the present moment. Fire tenders are expected to perform under similarly stressful and unpredictable conditions. How do we begin well? How do we arrive in ways that put us in a frame of mind to truly be with others? What are the practices and rituals for coming into a meeting space that support a grounded presence, clear purpose, and authentic way of leading? There are four categories of practices for preparing to lead, and to engage in them you must:

- Connect with the self

- Connect with the space

- Connect with the participants

- Connect with a larger world

Why Practices for Preparing to Lead?

As with world-class athletes, what happens just prior to our big events makes a world of difference in how we show up. What we do before the meeting can either support or undermine our effectiveness during the meeting.

What makes arriving practices so powerful? *Proximity* and *context*. Most of these practices are done on the day of a meeting, so if the practices positively affect our internal state, we carry that mental, emotional, and physical way of being into the meeting. Second, many arriving practices are done in the space where the meeting will take place. In a sense, the entire meeting space becomes an extension of our practice and a visual cue of the things we want to remember and hold close to us as we lead. Reciting my affirmation at home the day before the meeting is great. Reciting it in the meeting room thirty minutes before the meeting transforms me and the space into the vehicles through which my affirmation will come true.

Connect with the Self

Before the meeting it's easy to focus on logistics and the agenda. This is a mistake. Just prior to the meeting at least 50 percent of our focus should be on affirming who we need to be in order to help the group achieve its purpose. This is because *who* shows up as the meeting convener is as powerful an intervention as any technique or methodology.

You may be thinking, "I already know who I am, and I don't need to be reminded before a meeting." But high-combustion meetings have a way of disorienting us, often leading us to abandon our inherent wisdom, convictions and purpose.

Practices aimed at connecting you with yourself remind you of who you are, where you come from, and what you aspire to contribute in the meeting. Taking time to connect with yourself just prior to the arrival of participants serves a number of specific purposes. It will:

- Review and affirm your guiding intention for the meeting. (Remember that your guiding intention encompasses answers to such questions as, *Why am I here? Who am I here to serve? What are the principles that will guide me?*)

- Remind yourself of your hot buttons that might be pushed during the meeting and affirm your commitment to make deliberate choices in those moments.

High-combustion meetings have a way of disorienting us, often leading us to abandon our inherent wisdom, convictions and purpose.

- Remind yourself of the talents, insights, and gifts you have to offer the group.

- Put your ego and your attachment to outcomes in perspective.

- Check in with your body for any signals of unconscious fears, unhealthy attachments, or distractions.

- Invoke the wise, supportive, inspiring advisers in your life and the lessons they have taught you.

- Establish an inner and outer state of calm, clarity, and resolve.

Ideally, try to arrive before anyone else has come into the space. If this is not possible, set aside time for quiet introspection before you leave your home or hotel. Alternatively, there may be a quiet corner of the conference center, an alcove of the hotel lobby, a park or garden, or a nearby coffee house. Over the years, the time I take for introspection just prior to a meeting has become so important that if there are no other options, I will take refuge in my car or a toilet stall for even five minutes of final centering.

Practices for connecting with the self include some of the ongoing practices explored in the previous chapter—centering, meditating, and self-inquiry. Specific examples of practices that help leaders connect with the self are described below.

REMEMBER WHO IS STANDING BEHIND YOU

The process consultant Chris Grant says that during his pre-meeting ritual, he will ask himself who he needs standing behind him. Depending on the particular challenges he anticipates facing, he says, "it could be my mom or Nelson Mandela—and trust me, they are a formidable pair."[1] Here is how Chris described the practice:

1. Choose two to four people (they can be dead, alive, heroes, teachers, friends, or whoever else you want) that you need in the room today.

2. Close your eyes and mentally position them around the edges of the room.

3. Take a moment and let each of these people speak and declare your gifts and abilities.

GROUND YOURSELF IN YOUR GUIDING INTENTION

Grounding yourself in your guiding intention connects you with what's really important before a meeting.

Find a quiet place to stand, if possible outdoors or in front of a window so that you feel connected with the sky and the ground. Stand with your knees slightly bent, legs shoulder-width apart, and rest both hands on your belly just above your navel. Take a minute or two to feel the soles of your feet firmly in contact with the ground. This is the solid ground of your intention. Then silently review four questions:

What am I here to contribute in the world?

Who am I here to serve today?

What is the purpose I am here to help them achieve?

What principles and beliefs will enable me to lead with integrity and in the spirit of service?

This practice enables me to remember what I stand for. It sensitizes me so that I notice when I have stepped out of integrity during the meeting. And when I feel triggered or confused, I can consciously reengage both feet on the ground, place a hand on my belly, and know what I need to do next. These moves are not noticeable to others, but they help me reconnect with my guiding intention.

The negotiator William Ury described the importance of this practice in his own work: "Before any meeting I try to take time to slow down and connect with my bigger purpose. I am a devotee of peace, not as an outcome but as a process. This is my center. So in moments when people are shouting, I experience it as freedom. In the heat of these moments a calmness comes over me because I know why I am there."[2] Because Ury goes into each potential encounter with fire having clarified what he stands for, he is less likely to get grabbed by anxiety and ego.

Connect with the Space

I try to be the first to arrive in the meeting space whenever possible. Whether it is a traditional four-walled conference room, a virtual space on a conference call, or a large tent in a mountain meadow, any gathering space for me represents *awaiting*. The space awaits the people and the potential of what they might accomplish through their collaborative efforts. The meeting space provides comfort, establishes context, and sometimes offers inspiration for the work that's taking place within it. In that sense, the physical space in which I am working is my partner.

Seasoned meeting conveners invest a lot of time and effort tending to the physical space in which their gatherings take place. Many of those interviewed for this book say that the practice of setting up the space—moving tables, arranging the circle of chairs, hanging flip charts, and so on—is more than just a technical setup. It is an opportunity for us to establish a relationship with the physical environment and move into a deeper state of presence.

When we can appreciate the room as a three-dimensional screen through which to view the group, the room becomes a tool that we can use to see the meeting from different perspectives. Sometimes when I feel I am not seeing things clearly or am confused about what to do next, all I need to do is walk to another vantage point in the room to observe the group from there. Shifting my physical vantage point gives me a fresh way of seeing what is occurring and how I can contribute.

Some examples of practices for connecting with the space are described below.

BOW INTO THE ROOM

As described earlier, martial artists bow before entering and leaving the dojo, their practice space. One function of bowing is to remind ourselves that the space in which we are working is first and foremost a place of learning and practice. When we bow into a space, we acknowledge that we are learners. This simple act transforms the physical space into a constant reminder that we must approach the work of convening with humility and curiosity about what others might teach us during the course of the meeting. When we bow into the room, we are not disavowing our expertise; rather, we are acknowledging theirs. Humility is about realistically understanding our limitations. We don't have to diminish our gifts in order to express humility. With a single bow the meeting space becomes a visual reminder about standing with an open mind.

MINDFULLY ARRANGE THE SPACE

Whether the meeting begins in a circle or some other configuration, the act of arranging the chairs and other furniture can be as much an internal practice as it is a pragmatic step in pre-meeting logistics. Setting the chairs mindfully can be our first act of welcoming members of the group. When we carefully tend to the physical space, we are grounding ourselves in a kind of stewardship and service to the group. We are affirming the idea that "I am here to serve the group's purpose today and no job is too small." For Beatrice Briggs, a facilitator based in Tepoztlan, Mexico, arranging the space is a process that helps her establish readiness: "It's part of the ritual of preparation. . . . Mostly, while I'm setting up the physical space, I'm walking through the meeting and imagining a good outcome."[3] When we are able to establish a relationship with the room and arrange it into a welcoming, functional space, we are able to show up with less distraction and clearer intention.

SIT IN THEIR SEATS

When you have arranged the room, spend time sitting in the participants' seats as you do a mental walk-through of the meeting. Try to imagine the meeting taking place and think about when group members might feel anxious, engaged, bored, tired, or energized. From their seats try to notice every detail of the meeting space—where the light is coming from; the location of doors, windows, and artwork; the room temperature; and so on. Sitting in their seats will help you look out onto the group later in the meeting and see what is happening with more empathy.

Connect with the Participants

My colleague Sherri Cannon has a rule: "A half hour before the meeting is scheduled to begin, I want to be finished with all room setup and preparation. I want to be completely focused on connecting with participants."[4] Sherri's rule reflects how important it is for her to establish a human connection with the strangers about to converge on the room. When we can establish an authentic human connection with others, we are weaving a social fabric that helps us stand with greater compassion and openness, especially if things become emotionally intense or personal. Convening a gathering is the most human form of leadership, and it requires a commitment to being in an authentic relationship with people, whether those relationships last an hour or a lifetime.

A handshake, a smile, and some conversation about one's life inside and outside the context of the meeting goes a long way in building goodwill. A real conversation moves us past stereotypes and into authentic relationship. It may also help in breaking the participants' preconceptions about who you might be. During our interview, Roger Schwarz described his primary motivation for introducing himself to each person before a gathering formally begins: "It's about, 'Hey, I'm a guy in this room, and you are another person,' . . . so the thing doesn't start on this formal note. It's comforting for me."[5] The practice of connecting with participants in advance of the formal start strengthens our capacity to be present, receptive, and compassionate.

The practice of connecting with participants in a way that has integrity is harder than it looks because it is informed by three principles—authenticity, presence, and a lack of personal agenda. First, when you introduce yourself, you must be *authentic*—with no false personas or impersonations of "the self-assured facilitator." Authenticity transcends all barriers.

Second, you must be *present* in that first interaction. In those early moments in the room there is a lot to be distracted by—room setup, mental preparation, and people calling for your attention. As you reach out to connect with people, make each person the only thing in your field of attention.

> The practice of connecting with participants in a way that has integrity is harder than it looks because it is informed by three principles— authenticity, presence, and a lack of personal agenda.

Finally, you must make this an interaction with *no personal agenda*. Your goal is not to get the person to like you, to credential yourself, or to form power alliances. The purpose of connection is to see the other person and to be seen. If you monitor yourself on these three principles, you will be amazed at how often you violate them in those early interactions with participants. Whenever I become aware that I am working a personal agenda or being less than authentic with people during the arrival period, it is a wonderful opportunity to reconnect with my guiding intention.

Connect with a Larger World

How do you place yourself and your work in the context of the larger world? In what ways does your work connect with a bigger view of the universe or a higher calling? What do you believe to be the limits of your control in this meeting and in life? What are the larger, unexplainable forces to which you are prepared to surrender? What do you tell yourself during times of great uncertainty, confusion, and fear? In what do you place faith? What do you feel deeply grateful for as you arrive? These questions transcend the intellectual and emotional dimensions of preparation. Some might call them spiritual questions.

Connecting with a larger world does not necessarily involve engaging in a religious ritual. This category of practice involves taking time to remember that the act of people gathering to work on problems and to find common ground is in and of itself deserving of veneration and wonder. Some people want to feel connected with their god in this practice. Others may not believe in God but want a practice that helps them cultivate a deep appreciation of the mystery of human creativity and a reverence for what it takes to collaborate on difficult issues. Still others want to take a moment to honor the lineage of teachers who have informed and inspired their work. Practices for connecting with a larger world invite us to put the image of ourselves in proper perspective—simultaneously seeing the realities of our limitations and the infinite possibilities of what might be achieved.

Examples of specific ways to connect with a larger world include spending time in nature, praying, meditating, and chanting. At least two-thirds of the leaders and conveners we interviewed have some form of spiritual practice that aids them in recognizing the sacred nature of human endeavor and provides them with strength in the face of uncertainty and fear. Taking time to recognize and appreciate the connection between our work and the larger world strengthens our capacity to take risks, be flexible in the face of the unexpected, stand with resolve when purpose and principles must be upheld, and remain in the here and now when all of our fear-based instincts are advising us to find the nearest exit.

HONOR, GRATITUDE, AND LETTING GO

One way to connect with the larger world is to place attention on the gifts, mystery, and glory in the everyday. A pre-meeting practice of gratitude has a way of nudging ego and fear to the side, making room for receptivity. We have looked at how cultivating a lens of gratitude strengthens our capacity to dance with surprises and helps us see unexpected events as gifts rather than inconveniences and disruptions.

This is a template for a personal meditation that can be used before a meeting or even during a break:

> *I honor the shared intention that people have for today's gathering, which is . . .*
> *As I prepare for this gathering, I am deeply grateful for . . .*
> *I recognize others who have or are currently engaged in similar efforts throughout the world . . .*
> *I acknowledge that . . . are beyond my influence and control today.*
> *As I let go of . . . I hold on to faith in the belief that . . .*

Whether through a practice of gratitude or prayer, connecting with a larger world helps place us into a larger context. As the leadership and spiritual teacher Robert Gass said, "We are but leaves blowing in the wind."[5] In other words, we must arrive at our meetings grounded in the belief that there is knowledge beyond our current knowing, there is influence beyond our current influence, there are possibilities beyond our current ability to see.

Making Preparation Practices Work

Try to have a practice in each of the four categories described above, and connect with the self, others, the space, and the larger world. However, the specific practice you choose should be based primarily on what you feel you will most need on that particular day. For example, if I notice that I am arriving in a mood of anger or resentment because of something that occurred earlier in the day, my practice for connecting with the self might be compassion breathing. If I am feeling particularly intimidated by the meeting participants because of their titles or fame, I might spend extra practice in connecting with them and focus my self-connecting practice on my purpose and convictions so that I do not lose my resoluteness in the face of any strong personalities in the room.

Many of the practices described in this chapter require a commitment to arriving early to the meeting space. Make sure you have access to it a few hours in advance of the meeting. If it is not possible to get into the meeting space early, be very intentional about creating the time and space to practice connecting with yourself and the larger world in advance of arriving.

PRACTICES FOR PREPARING TO LEAD PUT US INTO

the proper mental, emotional, physical, and spiritual state
for a meeting. Like great stage actors and athletes, masterful fire tenders are almost ritualistic in the way they invest
their time just prior to a meeting. Preparation practices are
all about *connecting*. When we connect with our guiding
intention and personal gifts, we come into the meeting
more confident and clear. When we connect with the physical space, we strengthen our capacity to stand in the here
and now. When we connect with the participants, we set
the stage for compassion and open-mindedness to show
up. In connecting with the larger world, we remind ourselves to let go and embrace surprises.

QUESTIONS FOR REFLECTION

- What pre-meeting practices and rituals currently
  strengthen your ability to be an effective fire tender?

- What new practices for connecting with yourself just
  before the meeting starts might you consider?

- What new practices for connecting with the physical space
  might you consider?

- What new practices might assist you in establishing a
  more authentic and human connection with the people in
  the groups you facilitate?

- What new practices would assist you in connecting with
  the larger world or the spiritual dimension of your work?

FACE THE FIRE

When things heat up, it takes moment-by-moment awareness and adjustment to what you are feeling, thinking, and doing in the group. A brief lapse of awareness, and you can really set the process back.

—Myrna Lewis

Facilitator, Deep Democracy

MASTER FIRE TENDERS DON'T necessarily get triggered any less than others. But like championship ice-skaters, they seem to recover from missteps and falls more quickly and gracefully than the average leader. Most of the time, the in-the-moment self-correction occurs instantaneously, so that only the fire tender knows it occurred.

The self-directed practices in this chapter are specifically for use *during* meetings—in the heat of challenging events and difficult group dynamics. These practices for facing the fire assist us when we notice ourselves being pulled into a reactive or unbalanced state of being.

Why Real-Time Practices for Facing the Fire?

It is inevitable that at some point you will experience any number of strong thoughts and emotions—confusion, anger, fear, self-doubt, self-righteousness—on which you will be tempted to act. Practices for facing the fire are specifically aimed, first, at disrupting the natural impulse to act on those thoughts and feelings and, second, at replacing habitual reactions with more constructive responses.

You will find it difficult to have success with the practices in this chapter unless you have established the kinds of consistent, intentional, ongoing practices described in chapters 9 and 10. The first three practices—*attend*, *name*, and *pause*—are essential to master, and they are aided by the ongoing practices of body centering and mindfulness meditation. The fourth category of practices calls for you to *shift your state*. It offers approaches to modifying your mental and emotional outlook in the face of being triggered.

Attend

This first category of practice is one we became acquainted with earlier as part of the centering practice. The goal of attending is simply to notice what we are experiencing from moment to moment. Too often in high-intensity situations we become disembodied: we function completely in our heads and become cut off from any physical sensation. Disembodiment is a form of numbness. When we become disembodied, we no longer have access to the resource of our body as a key informant.

Attending to our physical sensations at regular intervals enables us to be present with the full experience of the moment. Attending also enables us to return to a familiar centered state from which we can begin all of the other practices described in this chapter.

Name

As we take stock of our physical state, we may sense discomfort, imbalance, or even pain. These are often indications that we've been emotionally triggered. *Naming* is shorthand for acknowledging that we have been triggered and for identifying the feelings and judgments we are having in the moment. For example, I might notice that my hands are clenched or my heart is racing. This enables me to name that I am feeling anxious.

The quicker we are able to realize that a hot button has been pushed, the sooner we can do something productive with it. The longer we go in a triggered state without being aware of it, the more likely we are to act from defensiveness and reactivity.

We need to know the telltale signs associated with being triggered because, as Robert Gass jokingly says, "when we get triggered, we are emotionally stupid."[1] In other words, when we are caught up in an emotional reaction, we are less resourceful and deliberate—and less likely to take action that serves the purpose of the meeting. Naming requires that we become intimately familiar with our own unique warning signals. Common ones include muscle tension in the neck and jaw, spaciness or numbness, feelings of resentment and blame, and repetitive thought patterns, particularly about what should and should not be happening. The practices for cultivating everyday readiness increase our capacity to recognize the telltale signs that we have been triggered.

When we encounter an uncomfortable physical or emotional state, the most basic question is often the most helpful: *What's up with me?*

Notice that the question is not "What's wrong with me?" When we name what is happening, we want to avoid making judgments about whatever is behind our reaction. It is simply happening. It is not good or bad, smart or stupid, mature or immature.

By naming, we take much of the power away from the reaction. We may identify that we are feeling defensive, worried about how we are perceived by the group, mired in self-doubt, or resenting a certain participant. In naming, our goal is not to suppress the feeling but to defuse its power.

When we encounter an uncomfortable physical or emotional state, the most basic question is often the most helpful: What's up with me? Notice that the question is not "What's wrong with me?"

Pause

When we feel on the spot and caught up in the drama of the group, our natural response is to act immediately in order to get the ground back under our feet—to restore our sense of control and safety. But just because we get hit with a strong emotion doesn't necessarily mean we need to take action. Pausing involves experiencing and appreciating this energy—observing it but not acting on it. The pause is a conscious choice not to act on the voice of self-protection and impulsiveness. This pause can last a second or several minutes. Pausing does not signify a passive stance. Though from the exterior we may appear to be doing nothing, we are in a highly alert and present state. This state of relaxed alertness is one that we cultivate through the mindfulness meditation practice. From this state of stillness, we are able to be curious, to see more clearly the choices available to us, and to discern more accurately what the group needs.

Pausing can be particularly challenging when we are facilitating a group that is looking to us for leadership, because it involves resisting the temptation to jump into the fray and "fix" the problem or make the discomfort go away. People project a lot onto us because of the authority that comes with our role. The challenge in moments of heat is not to validate their projections but rather to pause. In contrast to the suppression of our feelings, pausing involves restraint—experiencing anxiety, anger, or confusion but not acting on these feelings.

The moment of pausing is like standing at the crossroads of two responses. The first road leads to a defensive or ego-induced response. The motivation is psychological comfort. The second road leads to wise and deliberate choice. Attending and naming practices get us to the crossroads and offer us the choice. But we have spent so many years of our lives taking the first road that we are often not aware of the second.

The centering pause locates us in a space that is less cluttered with mental chatter, perceptual distortions, and emotions. It is a position of readiness from which we can deliberately shift into a more productive state.

Shift Your State

Having made the choice to pause, we are now in a more present state and are in a position to shift the attitude, emotion, or mood that is getting between us and tending the fire.[2] We can choose a wide variety of in-the-moment self-directed interventions. The purpose of these practices is to disrupt old habits by replacing them with something that is either neutral or more productive than our default reactions. These practices shift us into a way of being that is more aligned with our guiding intention.

BREATHE . . .

AND BREATHE THROUGH

When in doubt or distress, breathe.

The simple act of conscious breathing is an essential intervention. Breathing moves oxygen into the parts of our body denied by the fight-or-flight reaction. Intentional breathing gives us a single point of focus, enabling us to center ourselves away from a default reaction and back toward the purposeful self.

The practice of deep breathing is the first and quickest line of wise and responsible action in moments when we feel ourselves being triggered. Conscious breathing can be used in conjunction with the pause described above. When we breathe through while pausing, the breath serves as a focal point, strengthening our capacity for restraint. When in doubt or distress, breathe.

EVOKE A QUALITY

Developed by Wendy Palmer, this practice involves choosing a quality that we want to embody.[3] The purpose of this practice is to disrupt a default reaction by offering an alternative way of being in the moment. The quality we choose may be one that we are working on over a period of time. Some facilitators have a short list of qualities they find helpful to evoke in high-heat situations. As Palmer describes, evoking a quality requires just two steps:

1. Pick a quality you would find useful to evoke in the situation. For some hints, look back through the various ways of standing and capacities identified in part II.

2. Complete the following question, and answer it: If there were more *[name the quality]* in my *being, what would it feel like?*

When you become triggered and need to evoke a quality, construct the appropriate question for yourself. Hold it in your mind or say it out loud if you can find a moment alone.

So, having been triggered and feeling a need to control the situation, we might evoke the quality of fluidity by asking ourselves, "What would it feel like if I had more flexibility in my being?" In various moments we might ask for more openness, courage, clarity, patience, energy, humility, and so on. The art of this practice is selecting just the right quality in the right moment.

Notice that this practice involves asking a question rather than making a "should" or "should not" statement. Asking a question opens us to the possibility of what might happen next. As Wendy Palmer writes, "This 'not knowing' is the state from which intuition and creativity arise."[4] Evoking a quality is a direct path to any of the six ways of standing and a way to return to responsible stewardship of the meeting.

RECONNECT WITH YOUR GUIDING INTENTION

We have looked at the importance of standing with a clear guiding intention—knowing what we stand for. Reconnecting with a guiding intention is a particularly useful practice when we are sensing that things have moved off track in the meeting or that we or others are not operating within the boundaries of important guiding principles. We might experience this as guilt, confusion, or anxiety. In other cases, we may be enjoying the power or status the group has conferred on us while inadvertently stepping beyond the boundaries of our role. Whether the feelings are uncomfortable or pleasurable, we may intuitively sense that our integrity or the integrity of the meeting is slipping away.

There are many ways to reconnect with a guiding intention. The most straightforward is simply to ask ourselves a series of questions. When you're feeling confused or distracted by what is happening in a meeting, ask yourself these three questions:

Who am I here for, and what is their purpose?

What is my job and what is not my job in this setting?

What has integrity for me right now?

If we have not done the work of preparing in ways that ground us in our guiding intention, these are difficult questions to answer in the moment. However, if we have done the proper contracting with ourselves and with the group from the outset, this reconnecting process takes a matter of seconds. I can remember using this practice in a meeting in which I could see that the decision-making process had become corrupted. Three advertising agencies were competing for a large contract. The selection committee was made up of stakeholders, and some of those stakeholders let on during a break that they had been given expensive gifts by one of the competing agencies. It appeared that the bribing agency would be awarded the contract despite hard data that it did not meet the selection criteria as well as the other two candidates.

I had only a few minutes to decide what to do before the vote. Those three questions came to mind, and my answers were: My purpose is to help the group's highest wisdom emerge. I am here to serve the company's interests by facilitating a fair and rational process. Integrity means not pretending that I don't know what I know. Thirty seconds later I was calling for a break and informing the CEO of the information that had come to me. The decision was temporarily halted, and the bribing agency ultimately eliminated from the process.

A second, less cognitive way to reconnect with purpose and intention is a variation of the preparation practice used to ground yourself in a guiding intention. This practice involves a specific way of standing with your hands placed just above the navel. When you feel disconnected from your purpose, you can take a shoulder-wide stance, bend your knees slightly, and place a hand on your belly. Others will be unaware that you are inducing a state of heightened awareness and physically locating your internal gyroscope.

CHANGE YOUR PHYSICAL STANCE

We have been taught that body, mind, and heart are distinct domains and that we need to think our way into new emotions or physical moves. But as the leadership coach Chalmers Brothers writes, "All three aspects are connected to each other, reinforcing each other, striving toward consistency with each other."[5] In other words, our physiology can be the starting point for more productive thoughts or feelings. How we sit, stand, or walk, where we place ourselves in relation to others, our facial expressions, can all serve as gateways into the emotional and mental shifts we seek.

For example, my shoulders tend to fall forward naturally. But I slouch more than usual when I am feeling discouraged, closed, and judgmental. Over the years I have learned that I don't need to consciously try to change my attitude. I just need to pull my shoulders back and open my chest. When I do this, something shifts. It's as if my mind and heart are not capable of living with the incongruity I have created through my body. In the same way, when I feel emotional intensity sweeping me off my feet, I focus on the way the bottoms of my feet are in contact with the ground. When I feel anxiety or fear taking over my authentic sense of humor or playfulness, I make a point of wiggling my toes. Nobody knows that there is a little party happening inside those nicely polished loafers, but somehow, the movement shifts me into a different way of being.

During your next few meetings, experiment with your physical way of being and notice how your mindset and emotional state shift almost instantaneously.

- Feel the soles of your feet in contact with the ground.

- Pull your shoulders back and open your pelvis.

- Relax your jaw and lift your head.

- Straighten your back, extending the top of your head toward the sky.

- Smile.

- Let your in-breath go all the way down to your belly.

- Change the volume and tone of your voice.

- Stop talking.

Those are just a few examples of small physical adjustments you can make in the moment that may elicit a change in your mood and attitude. Try them all and experiment with more of your own. And remember, it's very hard to be fearful when you are wiggling your toes.

REFRAME THE SITUATION

The practice of reframing, also known as "cognitive restructuring," was initially described by the psychologist Paul Watzlawick.[6] The purpose of reframing is to help us see a troubling situation from another angle and, in seeing it differently, to widen the choices we have for responding. Reframing requires that we step back from our interpretation and ask:

> How else can I think about this situation and what I am doing in it?
> What other stories might I tell myself about it?
> What positive intent, explanation, or implication might underlie this situation?

These questions enable us to take off the "glasses" of our default ways of interpreting situations and inspect the lenses. We may find it less useful to ask whether an interpretation is true or false than to ask, *Is it useful in this moment?* When we reframe a situation, we find an alternative way of seeing the same facts. The situation remains unchanged, but our perspective is transformed.

Reframing illustrates how language is the primary way humans create meaning. When triggered, we are prone to catastrophize ("This disagreement is going to derail the whole meeting"), personalize ("And it will be all my fault"), assume the situation will be permanent ("And we'll never be able to get this group back on track"), and make pervasive conclusions ("These kinds of meetings just don't work"). Reframing offers alternatives to these self-defeating narratives.

The more practiced we become at reframing in the moment, the more quickly we are able to shift into a more responsive and productive state. We might in one moment feel overwhelmed by the group's long list of complicated and emotionally charged issues. We might be thinking, "You'll never be able to come to an agreement on how to tackle these issues." And in the next moment we might be able to think or even say out loud, "It's great you are talking about these challenges. It means you have the courage to bring them to light and the will to work on them. That's a big step."

As we come to know our personal hot buttons, we can anticipate some of the self-limiting narratives that will hook us. For these familiar narratives, we can have new frames loaded up and ready to use. For example, when I see someone "shouting" at others, my default story is "That is a rude, disrespectful individual from whom other people need protecting." If I buy my initial story, I might treat such a person with aggression or in some way overreact in the name of protecting the other group members. The problem is that my interpretation is often incorrect because my seeing is clouded by my habitual reaction to anger. I know that I need to have alternative frames in my back pocket so that I can use them to shift myself into a more effective state of being. So now, when someone raises a voice in anger, I quickly say to myself,

"Looks like this issue is really important to her" or "I see that he is doing his best right now to express his suffering."

Another reframing I have found to be useful moves me out of a narrative of victimhood ("They are messing up my meeting, so I'm forced to crack the whip") and into a narrative of choice ("I am choosing to hold stricter boundaries in service to the group's purpose"). Reframing limiting narratives in these ways helps us challenge our assumptions and gives us access to additional options for action.

MAKE USEFUL DISTINCTIONS

The more distinctions we can make, the greater our capacity for effective action. For example, Moi is a Huaorani Indian who lives in the Ecuadorian Amazon rain forest. When I walked through the forest with Moi, he could not only name the plants but could also recite the uses of each component of the plant—"We use the sap from this vine to treat wounds, and this tree bark we use for tea, and this leaf we use to make the roof of our huts." If I walked through the same forest by myself I would see lots of pretty plants. Moi sees things most of us can't see. And because of this, he has a much greater capacity for taking effective action in the domain of the forest.

Likewise, the more distinctions we can make regarding our interior landscape and the group dynamic, the greater the possibilities we have for making effective choices in the domain of high-heat meetings. Trying to lead high-heat groups without distinctions is like trying to survive in the Amazon basin for a week without Moi's eyes.

What distinctions help us recover when we become reactive?

Intent versus impact. I have no way of knowing other people's intentions. Any story I make up about their intent is just that. I can only observe the impact of their behavior.

Occurrence versus explanation. There is what happened, and then there is the story I make up about what happened. Keeping these separate helps me stay in reality.

Supposition versus fact. Most of what I think I "know" as fact is actually opinion, supposition, and inference. I need to remember this.

Ignorance versus blindness. Ignorance consists of the things we know we don't know. Blindness consists of the things we are unaware we don't know. The key is to be alert to the fact that we all have blind spots.

One of the most common distinctions people fail to make is between *differing* viewpoints versus *conflicting* ones. People waste immeasurable time in meetings because they get into debates about different perspectives, not realizing that those perspectives are not incompatible and can be easily combined. A fire tender alert to this distinction will be less susceptible to this unnecessarily divisive dynamic and can aid the group in finding common ground.

The key to this practice is to make distinctions part of our internal and external language.

When we can make these distinctions in the moment, we make more precise meaning out of challenging events and are therefore able to prevent our escalation into a reactive state.

CALL ON YOUR ALLIES AND ADVISERS

Many of the leaders we interviewed have very specific images of teachers, wise counselors, and inspirational people that they carry in their heads and hearts. If we have a ongoing practice focused on remembering these people and the lessons they have taught us, their counsel can be quickly accessed. When we need to make a quick shift into a more responsive way of being, we can ask ourselves:

What would this person do?

How would she see the situation?

What is he whispering in my ear right now?

For example, my dad's first cousin Sidney was a professor of social work in England and lived through his eighties. He was an important mentor to me, someone whose lessons I still carry. He used to say, "Larry, you have to remember that when people act angrily they are really just scared." Sidney's words are useful, but when I summon up his presence, I can also hear his reassuring voice. I see his playful smile and the twinkle in his eyes. I feel the confidence he had in me. Beyond remembering the lessons he taught me, conjuring up Sidney in my mind brings me into a place of calm and compassion.

Who are your teachers, supporters, and interior counselors—dead or alive? What are the lessons and forms of support they have given you? Train yourself to have the images of these people at hand. Make a list of three to five of your most important and inspiring advisers. Next to each of their names write down one or two sentences of their wisdom. Try to capture their teaching using words they might have used if they were speaking with you. Let this be the start of a "wisdom journal," which we will discuss in the next chapter.

USE AN AFFIRMATION

Affirmations are declarations or prayers oriented toward a positive outcome. Often the declaration is stated as if the outcome has already happened. Earlier we looked at personal affirmations as an ongoing practice. In the context of recovering *during* a meeting, an affirmation should not focus on the outcome of the meeting but, rather, on the state we want to be in to be of service to the group. So, we might say to ourselves, "I am the wide-open heart" if we want to shift our state toward more compassion.

An interesting variation on affirmations is the *Yes, And . . .* practice developed by Wendy Palmer.[7] This practice is specifically aimed at avoiding getting stuck in negative self-judgments and criticism. We might say, "I got really defensive with the group" or "I got intimidated and disappeared for a while" or "I misused my authority in that situation." The risk is that we remain in these states, doubting or blaming ourselves and being unable to shift.

Instead of trying to suppress or resist these negative messages, this practice allows us to acknowledge a mistake and then add an affirming aspiration that describes who we want to be moving forward. For example, "*Yes*, I misused my authority. *And* if there were more trust in my being, what would it feel like?" Here is the two-step process:

1. **Acknowledge** the negative message with a yes, taking in the true parts of the message in without resistance.

2. **Affirm** the quality or capacity you want to cultivate by adding *and* plus the question: "If there were more [of this quality] in my being, what would it feel like?"

This practice can be used to shift your state in the face of criticism that comes from yourself or the group. It helps you maintain compassion for yourself and a curious beginner's mind as you learn by making mistakes.

The aim of these in-the-moment practices for facing the fire is to move through a triggered state without taking regrettable actions, and then intentionally to shift into a way of being that supports your role as fire tender. In order to be truly useful, these practices must become second nature, like well-rehearsed dance moves. As masterful fire tenders, we can train our ears to hear the music of our own bodies and we can move fluidly into a series of practices that help poise us for clear and deliberate action.

Making Real-Time Practices Work

In the moment that you feel yourself becoming distracted or reactive, these real-time recovery practices make all the difference, especially if they are built on the foundation of the practices for cultivating everyday readiness and for preparing to lead. Getting good at using these practices means putting yourself in high-heat situations so that you can see how these practices work when you feel the pull to act on strong emotions. Sometimes the conditions can be simulated, but in most cases, these practices come with on-the-job training.

Getting good at using these practices means putting yourself in high-heat situations so that you can see how these practices work when you feel the pull to act on strong emotions.

The challenge becomes balancing our desire for a rich, high-heat learning opportunity and the concern that we might get in over our heads too quickly. As a practical matter I suggest you begin by using everyday interactions with family members, friends, colleagues, and clients to practice these approaches to in-the-moment state shifting. The more you look for them, the more you'll find the opportunities to practice recovering when you are grabbed by everyday events.

You can also practice shifting your state when you are alone and notice yourself becoming preoccupied with unproductive thoughts or feelings like impatience, stress, self-doubt, anger, and self-righteousness. These situations can range from standing in a slow line at the bank to working on a tight deadline.

Remember that your opportunities to use these practices for facing the fire will most often take place in settings where others are observing you. Whether it's as simple as pausing for a while or evoking a quality in the moment, engaging in a practice can feel risky because other people witness your process. In many cases, we can be transparent about our process and, in doing so, help others learn to better cope with their own reactions. When you falter in front of others, unable to refrain from a default reaction, remember that a sense of humor, authentic humility, and a sincere apology go a long way toward repairing any damage.

DURING THE MEETING, IN THE VERY MOMENT WE become triggered, distracted, or confused, we need a way out of a default reaction. Practices for facing the fire help us to quickly recognize old patterns of defensiveness and to replace them with responses that foster clarity, calm, and courage. These practices disrupt the default reaction just long enough for us to shift into a different way of thinking and feeling—a way of *being* that is more consistent with our guiding intention. Practices for facing the fire are the real-time "moves" every fire tender needs to learn to make. And none of those moves will be effective unless we have created a foundation of practices for everyday readiness.

QUESTIONS FOR REFLECTION

■ What are the specific physical and behavioral warning signals that your hot buttons are being pushed? What are the more subtle signals that precede the ones you just identified?

■ Can you think of a time when you named the hot button that had just been pushed, or when you consciously noticed that you were having some kind of emotional reaction, and you made a conscious choice to say and do nothing? What came out of the space you created in that moment?

▨ What practices do you currently use to shift your state from a reactive one to a clear and more deliberate way of being? What elements of these practices have you found to be useful? Which of the practices described in this chapter will you explore?

▨ In what ways do you notice that the practices for facing the fire are supported by the practices for cultivating everyday readiness from chapter 9 and the practices for preparing to lead from chapter 10?

REFLECT AND RENEW

There are rooms in my head I don't get to explore unless I spend time outdoors and with colleagues reflecting on my work.

—*Mary Margaret Golten*

Partner, CDR Associates

WHEN A MEETING ENDS, OUR intentional practices should continue. It sometimes feels as though we need every ounce of our physical, emotional, intellectual, and spiritual energy to create and hold together the container for a successful high-heat meeting. We need practices that support our sustained learning and renewal. The practices described in this chapter focus on what we do after the formal meeting has ended. They are practices in which you:

■ Leave it behind

■ Harvest the learning

- Celebrate

- Restore yourself

Why Reflection and Renewal Practices?

Practices that foster reflection and renewal enable us to relocate the center of our internal gyroscope and recommit to our purpose and convictions. They help us learn to more clearly see our habitual blind spots and avoid repeating unproductive patterns. These practices enable us to clear our heads, put events into perspective, and reenergize body, mind, and soul. Reflection and renewal practices demand that we create space for quiet and stillness from which new insights and deeper wisdom emerge.

Leave It Behind

It's an understatement to say that some of what happens in high-heat meetings is intense and at times even disturbing. In the interviews for this book, professional facilitators and leaders often made statements like "If I'm not careful, it's really easy to absorb the emotions in the room and take them all home with me." In order to avoid this, many of us have developed practices for leaving our meetings behind.

LINGER AND TEND THE SPACE

As they say in Open Space Technology circles, "When it's over, it's over."[1] A corollary to that principle is: "When it's over for them, it's not quite over for me." Tending to the space can be just another logistical step—gathering up flip charts, putting chairs away, and so on. But for many of us, this time in the room as participants depart is a time to wind down, decompress, and shed any negative emotional residue.

Lingering and tending to the space can take on a meditative quality. As I move into post-meeting mode, I take a moment to intentionally center myself. If people come up to me to say thank you or ask a question, I try to provide my full attention. At the same time, I don't invite any more conversation than is necessary. As I'm gathering materials and packing up, I am very aware of my breathing. After I have packed all of my things, I make a point to rearrange the room into its original condition. Just as I want to leave the meeting free from any mental or emotional debris, so I try to leave the room free from material debris.

The practice of lingering and tending to the room need not involve any mental debriefing with myself or others. For me, this practice of returning the room to its original state is an act of affirmation that this particular meeting on this particular day is one in a web of interconnected conversations in the organization and in the world. When I put the space back in order, I am reminding myself that other groups have met in this space before us, another group will occupy the space tomorrow, and still others in the weeks to come. It is my way of putting things into perspective and remembering that my work is measured by more than any single meeting. Tending to the space is a final act of service and a way to part from the meeting with a sense of inner peace, wholeness, and perspective.

USE THE JOURNEY HOME

Some of us commute long distances in order to convene meetings. Others do their work within steps of home. Regardless of the length of the journey or the mode of transport, we can use this trip to be intentional about reflection and renewal. A journey is the act of traveling from one place to another. This practice involves using the idea of "place" in a broader sense than geography. We can use our journey home to arrive in a different mental, physical, and emotional place.

Ask yourself, *What would serve my learning and renewal on the journey home?* For some, that journey is a time to smile and let some lightness into their being after a day of heaviness. For others, it's an opportunity to reflect on or write down thoughts so that they no longer occupy the mind. I don't tend to sleep well when I am traveling, so I often use the journey home to rest my body. For Chris Corrigan, the journey home is about moving from being a highly visible figure in a high-stakes meeting to blending back into the larger world. He describes it this way: "I love running a meeting, walking out the door, and walking into the street where I am just nobody again."[2] Whether your purpose is to rest, celebrate, or reintegrate into the world, making the journey home a mindful practice requires deciding what your intention is and how best to achieve that intention.

HAVE A CLEANSING RITUAL

If we allow our regrets, resentments, and nagging questions to accumulate after every meeting, they can begin to weigh us down in self-doubt, anger, and cynicism. We need a way to shed the day—to rid ourselves of the residual that still clings to us. Cleansing rituals are a great way to make this happen.

The cleansing ritual is most commonly an act of washing. It can be as simple as mindfully washing your hands at the end of a meeting or as elaborate as soaking in an herb-infused bubble bath accompanied by your favorite music. Marianne Hughes once described her cleansing ritual to me in this way: "For me, the bath is the physical action of letting go of the day, really caring for myself, and consciously resting and relaxing. It's literally letting this day go down that drain." There is symbolic power in the practice of post-meeting cleansing, and in the case of the bath, it can become a very practical act of self-care. However, we don't need water to cleanse ourselves of the day. Taking a brisk walk, reading a passage of poetry, or writing in a journal can have the same benefit.

CONVENE WITNESSES

The unusual and very powerful practice of convening witnesses after a meeting was shared with me by Zaid Hassan, a London-based facilitator and consultant. Zaid described an extremely difficult meeting in which members of his consultant team struggled with both the group's fire and their own reactions.[3] At the end of that meeting, the team invited three members of the group to come to another meeting to listen to the reflections of the facilitator team. Zaid recalls, "We said to them, 'We have been serving you for the last few days. We want you to hear our experience, how we felt, and what we struggled with.'"

In this post-meeting gathering, the facilitators did not want to justify the choices they made or defend their actions. They simply wanted to be heard. Zaid explained to me that this practice was developed because the team realized that in the past they had returned home carrying with them some of the suffering and trauma from certain meetings. The trauma damaged the consultant team's dynamic, and the witnessing practice was a way to leave the trauma behind.

Convening witnesses in this way requires special care in the selection of those who will be the witnesses. They must be people who are willing and able to suspend judgment and listen attentively. The benefit of this practice is that it serves as a kind of verbal and emotional "cleansing" of traumatic events. The ability to name one's personal struggles and suffering and to feel seen and heard by others goes a long way in being able to leave a meeting behind.

Harvest the Learning

After a meeting, conscientious facilitators typically invest energy in improving their designs, techniques, and methods. They focus on acquiring greater knowledge and improving their skills and methods.

It's less common that they focus on their interior experience—their mental, emotional, and physiological state of being and the impact of that state on their effectiveness and on the group. Harvesting practices are a systematic way to ensure that we are working to build our capacity for self-awareness and deliberate choice-making in the fire.

DEBRIEF

Debriefing sessions involve sitting down with others and reviewing how the meeting went. Typical debriefing questions focus on our strengths, weaknesses, and suggestions for how to do things better in the future. A more comprehensive session aimed at exploring the impact of our ways of being might also pose questions related to our internal state, particularly during those parts of the meeting when the group struggled with confusion, conflict, or emotional intensity. Questions for such a debriefing might include:

- To what extent did I, as the facilitator, remain present, open, and curious?

- To what extent did I maintain clarity and focus on the purpose of the meeting?

- To what extent did I demonstrate flexibility when surprises occurred?

Post-meeting debriefings can involve the client conveners, meeting participants, co-facilitators, or other colleagues who were present. The focus is on posing questions and soliciting feedback. The feedback is intended to shed light on potential blind spots and to give us the ability to discover patterns that limit our effectiveness as fire tenders. Such a debriefing often leaves clients and others with new insights about themselves and an expanded sense of their inner resourcefulness.

Journaling is generally a private endeavor. People keep a journal in order to capture a wide variety of ideas and feelings. There are as many approaches to journaling as there are individuals. For fire tenders, some of the most useful types of journals include critical-events chronicles, wisdom journals, and hot-button diaries.

Journals that focus on *critical events* from specific meetings take the form of a sort of "ship's log" and capture observations and lessons learned from each meeting. This provides the journaler with an opportunity to notice patterns and themes. This kind of journaling is particularly useful for a writer who has specific learning goals.

For example, let's say you decide to try for a period of six months to become more flexible in the face of unexpected events. You might focus your post-meeting journaling on the moments during meetings when you were caught off guard and on the way you handled those moments. As you write about these events, you might make particular note of your physical, emotional, and behavioral response to surprises as they occurred during the meeting.

Journals that capture the *wisdom of others* are useful because they give us a tangible tool for keeping our "inner advisers" close at hand. As we come across important ideas, principles, stories, or quotes, we write them in the journal and refer to them regularly. Both the writing and the reviewing reinforce the principles and make the wisdom more accessible. Remember that profound wisdom can be found in the most unexpected of places. Over the years I have written into my journal insights from management gurus and psychologists. But I have also recorded profound insights from cowboy poets, small children, and taxi drivers. Keeping a wisdom journal requires us to be alert all the time for the next gem.

We cannot change what we cannot see. The purpose of a *hot-button diary* is to help us see and befriend our personal hot buttons over time.

Hot buttons are akin to personal demons, which are, as Tsultrim Allione writes, the things that disturb us, drain us of energy, and trigger us into unproductive reaction.[4] We try to suppress and control our demons. We often project them onto others.

Think of your hot-button diary as your "reflections on your projections." It functions as a place to record those things that tend to grab you and evoke resistance, defensiveness, or any other response that puts a wedge between you and your guiding intention.

The first step in this journaling process is identifying your emotional hot buttons. Here are some examples of the kinds of questions you can use to observe your hot buttons after a meeting.

- What emotional hot buttons did I encounter?

- Who did I become when my hot button got pushed? Where did I hold the experience in my body, and what was the physical experience? What were my emotions, thoughts, and behaviors when this hot button got pushed?

- What external events or situations triggered this hot button?

- What kinds of memories, beliefs, moods, or subconscious thoughts seemed to be connected with this sensitive place within me?

- What is the unmet need that is behind this hot button?

- What lessons might this emotional hot button have to teach me? What personal strengths and sources of wisdom might be embodied by this hot button?

Whether you are harvesting insights from critical incidents, wise teachers, or encounters with emotional hot buttons, you don't have to limit your expression to words. Journals are ideal places to draw, paint, and make collages. They can become gathering points for scraps of inspiration and tidbits of wisdom cut from magazines or pulled out of fortune cookies.

Blogging is a form of online journaling. It can be used in the same way as any of the journals mentioned above, but there is an important difference. They are generally accessible to the broad public or to an audience authorized by the blogger. Blogs are a wonderful way to share lessons learned, wisdom gathered, and personal stories with others in the field. Communities of practice are often formed around a blog. For an excellent example of personal reflections on the art of convening meetings and the internal growth associated with our work, see Chris Corrigan's "parking lot" blog (linked on http://www.larrydressler.com/).

CELEBRATE

Speed seems to matter a lot in the world these days. In our hurry, we don't pause to mark beginnings and conclusions. Seriousness also seems to matter a lot. We have convinced ourselves that the serious realities we face mean that we must become serious people—grim, joyless, and unsmiling. Sometimes it feels as though speed and seriousness have sapped celebration right out of our lives. But fire tenders must challenge these cultural norms and build celebration into their routine.

Fire tenders have much to gain through celebration. We get to connect with the things for which we are most grateful, and in doing so, we connect with our hearts to the humanity we serve through our work. Celebration helps us cultivate gratitude. It helps us treat ourselves and others with more compassion. Celebration honors our purpose, and it strengthens our resolve to continue pursuing that purpose. Finally, celebration is time when we adults can explore our playful, joy-filled, fluid, even childlike nature, and allow ourselves the freedom to dance, sing, and laugh.

The work we do is often worthy of celebration, and there are many natural opportunities to celebrate if we are alert to them. Why celebrate? Sometimes we celebrate just getting through the fire intact. But we can also celebrate a beginning—the choice that a group of people make to come together to wrestle with a central question, tough problem, or new possibility. We can also learn to celebrate small, incremental successes, like the decision of historical adversaries to spend a few hours together in the same room. We can celebrate fleeting acts of courage and authentic expression while they are happening. We can celebrate our own growth, whether in its painful or joyous form. We can celebrate the fact that we get to do this kind of challenging, important work and that we live where people are free to express their deepest, most controversial truths.

Most of us who do the challenging work of convening high-stakes meetings do it because we believe in the transformational nature of conversations and relationships. The trainer and leadership coach Sherri Cannon described eloquently how celebration nourishes her sense of calling to help people create a breakthrough in their lives. "If I move on from something magical too quickly, it is lost. It doesn't get to settle into my soul and feed me."[5]

When can we celebrate? We can celebrate before the meeting even begins. Often when I arrive and am doing the practice of connecting with myself, I take a moment for gratitude that I am physically well and able to do this work I enjoy so much. We can celebrate as the meeting is commencing. One of my colleagues always brings flowers or

Sometimes it feels as though speed and seriousness have sapped celebration right out of our lives. But fire tenders must challenge these cultural norms and build celebration into their routine.

some other natural object into her meeting rooms as a way to celebrate beginnings, growth, and the larger context of life that is going on while the meeting is taking place.

We can also mark important moments during meetings. This can be as subtle as a silent acknowledgment and a smile to oneself for doing a nice job. It can take the form of spoken gratitude: "It took a lot of courage for you to put these issues down on paper and identify them publicly."

We can certainly celebrate in less constrained ways after meetings are over—whether alone or with participants, colleagues, friends, and family members. Sherri Cannon says, "The 'after' celebrating is for me about allowing what has happened on a human level to have my attention a little longer. Usually this celebrating happens when I'm alone. In that case, I write notes about the 'aha moments,' or I tell my husband, Roger, about it when we talk."[6]

Develop a set of celebration practices. Be creative and give yourself permission to be slow and inefficient about your celebrating. Put people in your professional and personal world who understand the essential value of celebration and let them serve as "celebration advocates," as my friend Sherri has done for me.

Restore Yourself

For some of the leaders and facilitators with whom I spoke, a high-heat meeting is exhilarating and energizing. They leave feeling refreshed and full of life. For others, a meeting can be simultaneously satisfying and draining. When we conclude intense periods of work, we need restorative practices that bring us back to a state of full energy and strength.

As with most practices, the challenge is not in knowing the practice. The challenge is in doing it. As you review these practices, ask yourself which might make the biggest positive difference in your work.

REST

To consciously or unconsciously deny oneself rest is to be on a path toward illness, burnout, or both. We live in a culture that values accomplishment, tireless effort, and action taking. In our zeal to earn a living and to make a positive difference in the world, it is so easy to run from one meeting to the next. But without rest we lose our ability to think clearly and our capacity to bounce back from the moments in which we get knocked off our feet by a group's intensity. First and foremost, rest means sleep. Second, rest means getting away from the mental demands of work and losing ourselves in other kinds of activities and relationships.

Many of us do work that involves sleeping away from home, often in hotels. Take the time and care to make your hotel room a haven for your nightly renewal. Ask for a room on a quiet floor. Unpack your bags and put the luggage in the closet, out of sight. Experiment with bringing along items like your own pillow, a scented candle, familiar music, and your favorite bedtime tea. Stay in hotels where you can exercise, swim, or walk the neighborhood.

Rest matters. We can all recall times when we "slept on it" or "stepped away" from a difficult problem and saw it with fresh eyes when we returned to it. Unless the physical container you inhabit is rested, the fullness of your gifts will be available neither to you nor to the group with which you are working. Here are some examples of restorative practices used by fire tenders.

> In our zeal to earn a living and to make a positive difference in the world, it is so easy to run from one meeting to the next. But without rest we lose our ability to think clearly and our capacity to bounce back from the moments in which we get knocked off our feet by a group's intensity.

SPEND TIME WITH ART AND NATURE

"Music restores the soul," as the saying goes. So does exposure to inspiring visual art, theater performance, and film. In the same way, enjoying the beauty of nature is an act of restoration. These kinds of practices enable us to use multiple senses and to experience what it means to be present—in the here and now. As one facilitator noted in an interview for this book, "When I am witnessing a moving theater performance or looking up at a star-filled sky, I get this window into my little place in the world. I get to see how small I am and how important I am all at once."

Mark Hodge, another facilitator, spends time in his rooftop garden in Delhi, India, which he describes as "a city that's not necessarily hospitable to cultivating plants." Mark reflects, "Some of the lessons I learn in my garden translate directly into my work with groups—patience, a long-term view, attention to subtle details of the environment, and a willingness to get my hands dirty." Art and nature feed the soul in ways that nothing else does, and because of this, they represent essential tools in the restorative process.

ENGAGE IN PHYSICAL PRACTICES

The physical practices described by people we interviewed include activities like swimming, running, walking, martial arts, rowing, cycling, hiking, dancing, and yoga. The primary purpose of these activities is to engage and challenge the body in a way that is enjoyable while achieving certain physical benefits like flexibility, balance, agility, stamina, and strength. All these physical benefits assist us when we are working in long, often grueling meetings. In addition, physical practices provide an opportunity to leave our mental chatter behind as we concentrate on the physical challenge. As one facilitator described, "I can be swimming for thirty minutes the night before a big meeting, completely focused on the rhythm of my stroke, and by the time I get out of the pool I have a new insight on how to handle the meeting." Physical practices help us condition our bodies and clear our minds in the service of becoming effective fire tenders.

ENGAGE IN CREATIVE PRACTICES

You don't have to be a Picasso or Pavarotti to pursue creative practices. These provide a haven from the more analytical side of our work. In the space of artistic expression, we are able to clear our minds and restore our energy. But creative practices do more than allow us to rest. They develop our ability to experiment, play with ideas, see new patterns, and take risks.

Like physical practices, creative practices let us get lost in them. Our interviewees named dozens of creative endeavors that are a consistent and nurturing influence in their lives. They include painting, dancing, playing an instrument, singing, collage, cooking, drawing, stone carving, improvisational acting, woodwork, photography, and gardening.

Creative practices encourage us to see the "ordinary" from a fresh vantage point as we apply our intuition, senses, and emotions to a task. When I am in my kitchen preparing a meal for friends, I am completely consumed by the activity. All of my senses are at play with the textures, temperatures, aromas, and flavors. I feel awake and joyful when I am cooking. How does this make me a better facilitator of high-heat meetings? The more I learn to trust my creative intuition in the kitchen, the more it translates to the meeting room. Cooking teaches me to work with messiness, dissonance, and surprises as welcome resources rather than problems to be fixed. When something I experience as distasteful shows up in my meeting, I accept it as one of many ingredients that may need a little more time in the oven. Most importantly, creative practices give us permission to make mistakes—to achieve new heights in imperfection and fallibility and to learn that today's "failure" holds the necessary insights that make tomorrow's masterpieces possible.

MAINTAIN A SOCIAL CIRCLE OF SUPPORT AND INTIMACY

We work every day in spaces filled with fascinating, motivated people, but somehow, our work can feel extremely isolating. We need a "home" that consists of close friends and family to whom we can speak our most difficult truths and share our proudest moments. Family members and close friends remind us who we are. More than anyone else in our lives, they are the candid and appreciative mirrors that reflect back to us who we are and who we are capable of being. In our meetings we must stay vigilant to our purpose. In the company of friends, we can rest in the warmth of their embrace and the pleasure of their company and just be.

LAUGH

Medical research shows that the health benefits of laughter include strengthening the immune system, reducing levels of stress hormones like adrenaline, and stimulating organ function. These health benefits are certainly relevant to us as leaders, but there are some less well-known reasons why laughter helps restore and strengthen our capacity to stand well in the face of difficult social interactions.[7]

Laughter provides a physical release for pent-up stress and emotions. A good laugh has a cleansing effect. It can be a beneficial temporary distraction from preoccupations associated with work, allowing us to return with a fresh perspective. Laughter can shift our mood, creating a more lighthearted way of seeing things. It engages our playful side, strengthening our capacity to see things from multiple perspectives. Most importantly, laughter has a way of connecting us with others. Its contagious nature often lightens the collective mood and improves the quality of social interactions.

As you develop restorative practices, look for ways to elicit laughter in yourself. Watch films and television programs that tickle your funny bone. Spend time with friends who bring out your sense of humor. And look for humor in everyday life. In moments that are particularly frustrating or challenging, look for the ridiculous or ironic elements and ask yourself, "Will I laugh when I look back on this?" Developing a well-honed eye for the absurd will not only serve you well during times of rest and renewal but will also serve you extremely well when you are standing in group firestorms and meltdowns.

LEARN FROM OTHERS

If we are awake, we are always learning. That said, involving ourselves in more structured learning is very useful in helping us acquire new insights and valuable tools for accessing our inner knowing. The ways in which we can learn from others include reading books, journals, and blogs; listening to audio lectures; attending in-person and online workshops; and spending time with mentors and in communities of practice.

However, people can spend thousands of dollars in workshops, tapes, or books and learn nothing. This is because learning is not an activity or event as much as it is an attitude. We need to choose our learning experiences mindfully and to enter them with openness. In the context of standing in the fire, the best kind of learning involves coming to know our thought patterns, physical sensations, and emotional land-scape more intimately. The Suggested Reading section at back of the book contains references for this kind of continued learning.

GO ON PERSONAL RETREATS

Lots of people in business don't like the word *retreat* because they asso-ciate it with retrenchment and defeat. I love the idea that we can give ourselves permission to withdraw from our routines and responsibilities, removing ourselves from the demands of our work and lives in order to renew and change our perspective. I also like the second meaning of *retreat*: a haven—a safe harbor from a storm.

Personal retreats take many forms. Diana Ho, one of my mentors and a master facilitator, takes a monthlong sabbatical each year, usually staying at home and dividing her time between doing her art, reflecting on the past, and planning for the future. Others spend time with mentors exploring their questions and articulating their aspirations. A personal retreat, on the other hand, has a number of unique characteristics:

It is self-focused. Because this kind of retreat is personal, it is aimed squarely at individual growth, renewal, and clarity. Even if other individuals are involved in our retreat (a coach or mentor, for example), we must not be burdened with responsibility for them.

It is nurturing. Any activities that might undermine our health and well-being or that deplete us physically, emotionally, or in any other way would be contrary to the purpose of a personal retreat.

It is not an escape. A retreat is not a vacation. On vacation we either vegetate or we busy ourselves with sightseeing and recreational activities. On retreats we engage ourselves and our questions. The questions we bring into a retreat embody its intention or purpose.

A personal retreat acknowledges that we are "instruments" of change. As the facilitator Rachel Bagby noted during our interview, "I go on personal retreats because I am an instrument and I need time to maintain the clarity and quality of my tone."[8] The "clarity and quality of our tone" is really another way of talking about our way of *being*. We can play the right notes in the prescribed rhythm, but the clarity and quality of the tone is what gives power to our music. Practices for reflection and renewal ensure that over the course of your lifetime the tone of your music becomes ever clearer and more beautiful.

Making Reflection and Renewal Practices Work

One of the great ironies of leadership is that we talk a lot about valuing sustainability and learning, yet our personal practices do not always reflect this value. This disconnect between what we say we value and how we live forces us to examine whether we are leading with integrity. As with ongoing practices aimed at preparing, *being* someone who has specific practices that focus on reflection and renewal is different from talking about it. There is no faking it. People sense the difference in a matter of minutes.

Before going into a challenging meeting, have a plan in mind for reflection and renewal. What will you do to leave the meeting behind? How will you harvest the lessons you must take away? What will you do to celebrate? How will you restore yourself physically, mentally, and emotionally after the meeting? Begin by experimenting with practices that fit within your lifestyle, but if you find that your existing routine does not permit time for reflection and renewal, seriously consider changes to your lifestyle to make room for these practices. They are fundamental not only to your work but also to a long and fulfilling life.

FIRE TENDING CAN BE CHALLENGING AND TIRING WORK. We need practices that foster our ongoing learning and renewal. Otherwise we become vulnerable to repeating ineffective patterns and burning out. Though we live in a culture that does not always encourage down time and celebration, practices for reflection and renewal must become as normal as brushing our teeth and as essential as breathing. Through these practices we become wiser, stronger, clearer leaders. These practices foster our continued growth and ensure rejuvenation so that we can continue to be carriers of wisdom and catalysts of positive change.

QUESTIONS FOR REFLECTION

- How do you know when you are in need of renewal? What are the signals that you need to rest and reenergize?

- What current practices do you have for reflecting on your experiences and harvesting the lessons learned after your meetings?

- How do you celebrate in your work and life? Where are the opportunities to more mindfully celebrate?

- What current practices do you have for renewing yourself physically, emotionally, mentally, and spiritually? What seems to have the greatest positive benefit?

- Which of the practices described in this chapter would offer you positive benefits in terms of sustaining your personal learning, growth, and well-being?

STEPPING INTO THE FIRE CIRCLE

FIRE TENDERS ARE MOTIVATED by the possibility that each conversation we convene might catalyze some small or large change in a world that's calling out for innovative, collaborative solutions. But we can't be true stewards of participation equipped only with the *what* of knowledge. We can't be catalysts for innovation, transformation, and healing armed solely with the *how* of group methods. We need to learn to be sources of calm, clarity, and courage in the face of group passion, conflict, confusion, and despair. We need to be intentional about *who* we are being and who we are becoming.

Each time we stand in the fire and encounter our ego, habitual ways of seeing, and emotional hot buttons is a new step in this odyssey of becoming. Recently, while facilitating a conference workshop for the International Association of Facilitators, I was having some difficulty calling people back together after a breakout session. Usually I carry a small bell with me, but I'd forgotten it in my hotel room and my voice was not carrying very well. I raised my hand, made a few loud announcements, and even switched the lights off and on in an attempt to corral the fifty participants. It was all to no avail.

People seemed animated and engrossed by their small-group conversations and clearly did not want to conclude the breakout session. I thought, "Either they don't notice me or they are ignoring me." I stood in the middle of the room noticing what it felt like to be invisible in my own workshop. I was the expert they had come to hear, and they had realized that the most profound insights of the day would come from one another.

Here was a moment of choice. I began to smile and then to laugh. I was smiling at the gift of their enthusiasm. I was laughing at myself—at the way my personal power and my limitations could coexist in the same moment and the fact that I had no idea what I would do next. I felt relaxed knowing that *what* I did mattered much less than *who* was showing up.

To be a fire tender is to know that you choose *who* you are being from moment to moment. You choose whether to dig in or dance with the trickster. You choose whether to stand with certainty or curiosity. You choose whether to place your attention on "then and there" or on "here and now." You choose to act from self-protection or from service. Fire tending is a journey of moment-to-moment awareness and choice. You can be a fire tender as you face the challenges of daily life just as readily as you can in the heat of a high-stakes meeting. All of life is your practice field.

As you embark on your own journey of inner discovery, I wish you the kind of laughter that grounds you in humility and the kind of clarity that emboldens you toward greater integrity and authenticity. I encourage you to be gentle with yourself when your learning is painful. I invite you to step into this circle with other fire tenders knowing that you are part of a larger community of peacemakers and catalysts for change. Step into the fire circle feeling the weight of your uncertainty and immense awe for the task at hand. And let your laughter be an encouraging companion whispering in your ear and reminding you always that this work of leading is a deeply human endeavor.

NOTES

PREFACE

1. Parker Palmer, *A Hidden Wholeness: The Journey Toward an Undivided Life* (San Francisco: Jossey-Bass, 2004), 47.

CHAPTER 1

1. Ellen Langer, *Mindfulness* (New York: Perseus Books, 1989).
2. Steven Johnson, *Mind Wide Open: Your Brain and the Neuroscience of Everyday Life* (New York: Scribner, 2004), 64.
3. Mark R. Leary, *The Curse of Self: Self-Awareness, Egotism, and the Quality of Human Life* (New York: Oxford University Press, 2004), 76.
4. Ibid.
5. Chris Corrigan, telephone interview with Erica Peng, January 2009.
6. Pema Chödrön, *When Things Fall Apart: Heart Advice for Difficult Times* (Shambhala Publications, Inc., 1997), 12.

CHAPTER 2

1. Georgia Warren, "Humans Drive Biggest Mass Extinction since Dinosaur," Sunday *Times*, October 26, 2008, http://www.timesonline.co.uk/tol/news/environment/article5014714.ece (accessed May 26, 2009).

2. Daniel Goleman, *Social Intelligence: The New Science of Human Relationships* (London: Arrow Books, 2007), 275.
3. Ibid.
4. Marianne Hughes, telephone interview with author, February 2009.
5. Edwin Friedman, *A Failure of Nerve: Leadership in an Age of the Quick Fix* (New York: Seabury Book, 2007), 183.
6. Marianne Williamson, *A Return to Love: Reflections on the Principles of a "Course in Miracles"* (New York: Harper Paperbacks, 1996), chap. 7, sec. 3.

CHAPTER 3

1. Paul Eckman, *Emotions Revealed: Recognizing Faces and Feelings to Improve Communication and Emotional Life* (New York: Times Books, 2003), chap. 2.
2. Ibid.
3. Ibid., 39.
4. Peter Block, *The Answer to How Is Yes: Acting on What Matters* (San Francisco: Berrett-Koehler Publishers, 2003), 4.
5. Richard Strozzi Heckler, *The Anatomy of Change: A Way to Move Through Life's Transitions* (Berkeley, CA: North Atlantic Books, 1993), 16.

CHAPTER 4

1. Consultant, telephone interview with author, January 2009. This consultant asked that the interview be conducted anonymously.

2. Linda Myoki Lehrhaupt, *T'ai Chi as a Path to Wisdom* (Boston: Shambhala Publications, Boston, 2001), 5.

3. Eckhart Tolle, *The Power of Now: A Guide to Spiritual Enlightenment* (London: Hodder & Stoughton, 1999), 48.

4. John Heider, *The Tao of Leadership* (New York: Bantam Books, 1986).

CHAPTER 5

1. Neil Postman, *The End of Education: Redefining the Value of School* (New York: Vintage Books, 1996).

2. Peter Senge, *The Fifth Discipline: The Art and Practice of the Learning Organization* (New York: Currency-Doubleday Publishing, 1990), 142.

3. Parker Palmer, "The Broken-Open Heart: Living with Faith and Hope in the Tragic Gap," *Weavings*, March-April 2009.

4. C. Otto Scharmer, *Theory U: Leading from the Future as It Emerges* (San Francisco: Berrett-Koehler Publishers, 2009), 42.

5. Hughes interview (see chap. 2, n. 4).

CHAPTER 6

1. Parker Palmer, *Let Your Life Speak: Listening to the Voice of Vocation* (San Francisco: Jossey-Bass Publishers, 2000), 4.

2. Robert Greenleaf, *Servant Leadership: A Journey into the Nature of Legitimate Power and Greatness* (Mahwah, NJ: Robert K. Greenleaf Center, 1977).

CHAPTER 7

1. Consultant interview (see chap. 4, n. 1).

2. Harrison Owen, *Wave Rider: Leadership for High Performance in a Self-Organizing World* (San Francisco: Berrett-Koehler Publishers, 2008), 1.

3. Consultant interview (see chap. 4, n. 1).

4. Kevin Cashman, *Leadership from the Inside Out: Becoming a Leader for Life* (Provo, UT: Executive Excellence Publishing, 1998), 80.

5. Margaret Wheatley and Myron Kellner-Rogers, *A Simpler Way* (San Francisco: Berrett-Koehler Publishers, 1998), 22.

CHAPTER 8

1. Alan Morinis, *Everyday Holiness: The Jewish Spiritual Path of Mussar* (Boston: Trumpeter Books, 2007), 75.

2. Susan Scott, *Fierce Conversations: Achieving Success at Work and in Life One Conversation at a Time* (New York: Berkley Publishing Group, 2002).

3. Mark Jones, telephone interview with Erica Peng, January 2009.

4. David Sibbett, telephone interview with Erica Peng, January 2009.

5. Ruben Perczek, telephone interview with the author, January 2009.

6. Myrna Lewis, telephone interview with the author, January 2009.

CHAPTER 9

1. Victoria Castle, *The Trance of Scarcity: Stop Holding Your Breath and Start Living Your Life* (San Francisco: Berrett-Koehler Publishers, 2007), 76.

2. Parker Palmer, *A Hidden Wholeness: The Journey Toward an Undivided Life* (San Francisco: Jossey-Bass, 2009).

3. Diane Robbins, telephone interview with Erica Peng, January 2009.

4. Chödrön, *When Things Fall Apart*, 122 (see chap. 1, n. 6).

5. Peggy Holman, telephone interview with Erica Peng, January 2009.

CHAPTER 10

1. Chris Grant, telephone interview with Erica Peng, January 2009.

2. William Ury, interview with the author, August 2009.

3. Beatrice Briggs, telephone interview with Erica Peng, January 2009.

4. Sherri Cannon, interview with the author, January 2009.

5. Roger Schwarz, telephone interview with the author, January 2009.

6. Robert Gass, interview with the author, June 2009.

CHAPTER 11

1. Gass interview (see chap. 10, n. 6).

2. Special thanks to Robert Gass for offering the lovely language of "state shifting" to describe this set of practices. Robert has been using and teaching these practices to leaders, activists, and couples for three decades. I interviewed Robert at his home in Boulder, Colorado, while researching this book.

3. Wendy Palmer, *The Intuitive Body: Discovering the Wisdom of Conscious Embodiment and Aikido* (Berkeley, CA: Blue Snake Books, 2008), 33.

4. Ibid.

5. Chalmers Brothers, *Language and the Pursuit of Happiness* (Naples, FL: New Possibilities Press, 2005), 141.

6. Paul Watzlawick, *The Language of Change: Elements of Therapeutic Communication* (New York: W.W. Norton, 1978).

7. Palmer, *The Intuitive Body*, 190.

CHAPTER 12

1. Harrison Owen, *Open Space Technology: A User's Guide* (San Francisco: Berrett-Koehler Publishers, 1997), 95.

2. Corrigan interview (see chapter 1, n. 5).

3. Zaid Hassan, telephone interview with author, January 2009.

4. Tsultrim Allione, *Feeding Your Demons: Ancient Wisdom for Resolving Inner Conflict* (New York: Little, Brown, 2008)

5. Cannon interview (see chap. 10, n. 4).

6. Ibid.

7. Elizabeth Scott, "The Many Benefits of Laughter," About.com, January 24, 2008, http://stress.about.com/b/2008/01/24/the-many-benefits-of-laughter.htm (accessed April 2, 2009).

8. Rachel Bagby, telephone interview with Erica Peng, January 2009.

SUGGESTED READING

STANDING WITH SELF-AWARENESS

Chris Argyris, *Overcoming Organizational Defenses: Facilitating Organizational Learning* (Englewood Cliffs, NJ: Prentice-Hall, 1990).

Chalmers Brothers, *Language and the Pursuit of Happiness* (Naples, FL: New Possibilities Press, 2005).

Mark R. Leary, *The Curse of Self: Self-Awareness, Egotism, and the Quality of Human Life* (New York: Oxford University Press, 2004).

STANDING IN THE HERE AND NOW

Thich Nhat Hanh, *The Miracle of Mindfulness* (Boston: Beacon Press, 1976).

Eckhart Tolle, *The Power of Now: A Guide to Spiritual Enlightenment* (London: Hodder & Stoughton, 1999).

STANDING WITH AN OPEN MIND

Arbinger Institute, *Leadership and Self-Deception: Getting Out of the Box* (San Francisco: Berrett-Koehler Publishers, 2002).

Ronald Gross, *Socrates' Way: Seven Master Keys for Using Your Mind to the Utmost* (New York: Penguin Putnam, 2002).

Ellen Langer, *Mindfulness* (New York: Perseus Books, 1989).

Shunryu Suzuki, *Zen Mind, Beginner's Mind* (Boston: Shambhala Publications, 2004).

KNOWING WHAT YOU STAND FOR

Peter Block, *The Answer to How Is Yes: Acting on What Matters* (San Francisco: Berrett-Koehler Publishers, 2003).

Wayne Dyer, *The Power of Intention: Change the Way You Look at Things and the Things You Look at Will Change* (Carlsbad, CA: Hay House, 2004).

Robert Greenleaf, *Servant Leadership: A Journey into the Nature of Legitimate Power and Greatness* (Mahwah, NJ: Robert K. Greenleaf Center, 1977).

Parker Palmer, *Let Your Life Speak: Listening for the Voice of Vocation* (San Francisco: Jossey-Bass, 1999).

DANCING WITH SURPRISES

Pema Chödrön, *When Things Fall Apart: Heart Advice for Difficult Times* (Boston: Shambhala Publications, 1997).

Harrison Owen, *Wave Rider: Leadership for High Performance in a Self-Organizing World* (San Francisco: Berrett-Koehler Publishers, 2008).

Margaret J. Wheatley, *Leadership and the New Science: Discovering Order in a Chaotic World* (San Francisco: Berrett-Koehler Publishers, 2006).

STANDING WITH COMPASSION

Richard Boyatzis and Annie McKee, *Resonant Leadership: Renewing Yourself and Connecting with Others through Mindfulness, Hope, and Compassion* (Cambridge, MA: Harvard Business School Press, 2005).

Pema Chödrön, *When Things Fall Apart: Heart Advice for Difficult Times* (Boston: Shambhala Publications, 1997).

Thomas Merton, ed., *Gandhi on Non-violence* (New York: New Directions, 1965).

MANY WAYS OF STANDING

Angeles Arrien, *The Fourfold Way: Walking the Paths of the Warrior, Teacher, Healer, and Visionary* (San Francisco: Harper Publishing, 1993).

Arnold Mindell, *The Leader as Martial Artist: Techniques and Strategies for Revealing Conflict and Creating Community* (New York: Harper Publishing, 1992).

Susan Scott, *Fierce Conversations: Achieving Success at Work and in Life One Conversation at a Time* (New York: Berkley Publishing Group, 2002).

William Ury, *Getting to Peace: Transforming Conflict at Home, at Work, and in the World* (New York: Viking, 1999).

INNER-DIRECTED PRACTICES

Tsultrim Allione, *Feeding Your Demons: Ancient Wisdom for Resolving Inner Conflict* (New York: Little Brown, 2008).

Julia Cameron, *The Artist's Way: A Spiritual Path to Higher Creativity* (New York: Penguin Putnam, 2002).

Victoria Castle, *The Trance of Scarcity: Stop Holding Your Breath and Start Living Your Life* (San Francisco: Berrett-Koehler Publishers, 2006).

Peter J. Frost, *Toxic Emotions at Work and What You Can Do about Them* (Cambridge, MA: Harvard Business School Press, 2007).

Richard Leider, *The Power of Purpose: Creating Meaning in Your Life and Work* (San Francisco: Berrett-Koehler Publishers, 2005).

Thich Nhat Hanh, *Anger: Wisdom for Cooling the Flames* (New York: Riverhead Trade, 2002).

Jon Kabat-Zinn, *Wherever You Go, There You Are: Mindfulness Meditation in Everyday Life* (New York: Hyperion, 1995).

Byron Katie, *Loving What Is: Four Questions That Can Save Your Life* (New York: Three Rivers Press, 2003).

Joanna Macy and Molly Young Brown, *Coming Back to Life: Practices to Reconnect Our Lives, Our World* (Gabriola Island, BC: New Society Publishers, 1998).

Parker Palmer, *A Hidden Wholeness: The Journey Toward an Undivided Life* (San Francisco: Jossey-Bass, 2009).

Wendy Palmer, *The Intuitive Body: Discovering the Wisdom of Conscious Embodiment and Aikido* (Berkeley, CA: Blue Snake Books, 2008).

Doug Silsbee, *Presence-Based Coaching: Cultivating Self-Generative Leaders through Mind, Body, and Heart* (San Francisco: Jossey-Bass, 2008).

GROUP FACILITATION SKILLS

Michael Doyle and David Strauss, *How to Make Meetings Work: The New Interaction Method* (New York: Berkley Trade, 1993).

Larry Dressler, *Consensus through Conversation: How to Achieve High-Commitment Decisions* (San Francisco: Berrett-Koehler Publishers, 2006).

Dale Hunter, Anne Bailey, and Bill Taylor, *The Zen of Groups: A Handbook for People Meeting with a Purpose* (Tucson, AZ: Fischer Books, 1995).

Sam Kaner et al., *Facilitator's Guide to Participatory Decision-Making* (San Francisco: Jossey-Bass, 2007).

Roger Schwarz, *The Skilled Facilitator: A Comprehensive Resource for Consultants, Facilitators, Managers, Trainers, and Coaches* (San Francisco: Jossey-Bass, 2002).

Marvin Weisbord and Sandra Janoff, *Don't Just Do Something, Stand There: Ten Principles for Leading Meetings That Matter* (San Francisco: Berrett-Koehler Publishers, 2007).

Web-Based Resources

The following online resources are available through the author's Web site at **http://www.larrydressler.com/**:

▓ Downloadable tools that support your learning as a fire tender

▓ Links to Web sites offering workshops that focus on inner-development

▓ Links to Web sites offering tools and practices that support the six ways of standing

▓ An updated list of recommended books by other authors

▓ Access to Larry Dressler's blog and downloadable articles

ACKNOWLEDGMENTS

THIS BOOK WAS BORN out of a forty-year conversation that I've been having with myself. It would have remained just that had it not been for Johanna Vondeling at Berrett-Koehler Publishers, who has been a friend, creative sounding board, and caring steward of this writing effort.

Many of the insights and stories in this book came from interviews with leaders and facilitators who live on five continents and who have dedicated their lives to improving the world by convening conversations that matter. I am proud to call them my colleagues and friends and am deeply appreciative of their wisdom and generosity. They are Margo Adair, Rachel Bagby, Ingrid Bens, Tree Bressen, Beatrice Briggs, Mary Campbell, Sherri Cannon, Chris Corrigan, Saul Eisen, Caitlin Frost, Robert Gass, Mary Margaret Golten, Chris Grant, Sono Hashisaki, Zaid Hassan, Diana Ho, Mark Hodge, David Hoffman, Peggy Holman, Marianne Hughes, Mark Jones, Dave Joseph, Adam Kahane, Stewart Levine, Myrna Lewis, Kenoli Oleari, Ruben Perczek, Diane Robbins, Gibran Rivera, Roger Schwarz, Sandy Schuman, James Shaw, David Sibbett, Doug Silsbee, Molly Tayer, Sera Thompson, William Ury, Sidney Wasserman, and Margaret Wheatley.

A special thanks to Peggy Holman for suggesting the term *fire tender* during our phone interview with her. Thanks also to Robert Gass for offering the language of "state shifting" to describe what we can do for ourselves when our hot buttons get pushed.

I am deeply grateful to Erica Peng, who so masterfully conducted most of the interviews and served as an invaluable thinking partner throughout the writing of the manuscript. The book is better and my life is richer for having worked so closely with Erica over the past year.

Thanks to those who so conscientiously reviewed drafts of the manuscript, illuminating my blind spots and providing suggestions— Andrea Chilcote, Chris Corrigan, Sam Elmore, Sharon Goldinger, Sharon Kipersztok, Karen Seriguchi, and Maren Showkeir.

Finally, to my wife, Linda Smith, who knows my authentic voice like no one else and has helped me learn to write in that voice. *Gracias, mi amor.*

ABOUT THE AUTHOR

MICHAEL BROOKS

LARRY DRESSLER HAS DEDICATED most of his life to understanding how people work out their differences, discover common ground, and mobilize collective action. As a young boy he attended schools where bullying, gang conflict, and violence were everyday occurrences. From an early age he learned to navigate the hallways and the larger world by deciphering subtle social dynamics and building resilient relationships.

Later in life Larry worked with youth in the low-income neighborhoods of South-Central Los Angeles and then as an assistant regional director for an international human rights organization. Over the years a central question emerged for Larry: What are the human qualities that enable one to bring peace, clarity, and hopefulness into situations that are filled with conflict, confusion, and despair?

Larry continues to embrace this question as a widely recognized organizational development consultant and process facilitator. He has consulted with hundreds of organizations, including Cisco, Pediatric AIDS Foundation, Baxter Healthcare, New Belgium Brewing, Starbucks, Nissan Motors, and 1% for the Planet. His extraordinary skill and presence as a "gentle instigator of breakthrough conversations" have brought him to such diverse settings as the headquarters of companies in thirty industries, a circus school in Colorado, a solar-powered chocolate factory in the Amazon rain forest, and an industrial disaster site in Washington State.

Larry's reputation as a master storyteller, entertaining speaker, and engaging workshop facilitator are evidenced by the many invitations he receives to make presentations at professional conferences, industry gatherings, and leadership retreats. He is the author of *Consensus through Conversation: How to Achieve High Commitment Decisions* (Berrett-Koehler Publishers, 2006), selected by *Training & Development* magazine as "one of the year's top ten books" in 2006 and recently translated into Chinese.

Today Larry invests his time helping leaders explore how to simultaneously achieve economic results, foster a more just society, and restore the natural environment. He also delivers keynotes and leadership development seminars internationally on Standing in the Fire™ and Fierce Conversations™.

Larry's formal education has enabled him to see the world through the lens of a social psychologist while speaking the language of business and strategy. He earned a BA from UCLA in sociology and an MBA from the UCLA Anderson Graduate School of Management.

Larry lives in Boulder, Colorado, with his wife, Linda Smith. Together they co-founded Reading Village, a not-for-profit organization that promotes children's literacy in rural Guatemala. You can visit his Web site at http://www.larrydressler.com/.

INDEX

centering. *See* physical centering.

Change Your Questions, Change Your Life, 135

Chavez, Hugo, anecdote, 89–90

Chödrön, Pema, 21, 140

Chouinard, Yvon, 136

clarity
anecdote, 89–90
knowing what you stand for, 89–90
preparing to lead, 152

cleaning up after a meeting, 181–182

cleansing rituals, after a meeting, 183

clearness committees, 137–139

closed hearts, symptoms of, 111–112

co-facilitators, partnering with, 144

cognitive restructuring, 171–173

coherence
anecdote, 93–95
knowing what you stand for, 91–92

combustibility, conditions for, 7–8

comfort zone, stepping out of, 143–144

commitment
to building personal practices, 147
knowing what you stand for, 90–91

community activists. *See* fire tenders.

compassion
benefits of, 121–122
healing, 121
journaling, 139–140
love, 122
overview, 114–116
trust, 122

compassion, potential problems
aggression, 113
apathy, 113
closed hearts, symptoms of, 111–112
professional detachment, 112–113
projections, 114
repression, 112–113

compassion, required capacities
awareness of the whole person, 119–120
emotional openness, 116–117
self acceptance, 117–119
unconditional positive regard, 120–121

compassion breathing, 140–141

confidence, dealing with surprises, 107–108

conflict resolution specialists. *See* fire tenders.

conflicting viewpoints *versus* differing, 174

connecting with
guiding intentions, 153, 158, 168–170
the larger world, 158–160
participants, 156–158
physical space, 154–156
the self, 50, 151–152

conscious thoughts, 44–45

consistency of personal practices, 126, 137, 141

consultants. *See* fire tenders.

contributing to the world, 85–86

control, need for, 98–100

convening
meetings. *See* meetings.
witnesses after a meeting, 184

core intentions. *See* guiding intentions.

Corrigan, Chris
blog, 188
the illusion of fire, 21
stakeholders, identifying, 87–88

courage
anecdote, 93–95
knowing what you stand for, 92

creative personal practices, 126, 193–194

creativity, and open-mindedness, 77

critical events, journaling, 186

curiosity
case studies and anecdotes, 75
open-mindedness, 74–75

Dalai Lama, 10

Dalai Lama Renaissance, 10

dancing with surprises. *See* surprises.

debriefing, after a meeting, 185

deeper knowing, 138

default reactions
defensive responses, 81
definition, 18
disrupting, 166–168
fleeing the situation, 112
deliberate choice and wise action, 2

differing viewpoints *versus* conflicting, 174

dignity, unconditional positive regard, 120–121

discovering what you stand for, 93–95. *See also* knowing what you stand for.

distinctions, useful, 173–174

diversity training workshop, anecdote, 61

Dressler, Larry, influences on, xv

Eckman, Paul, 39–41

ego
influence on identity, 19–20
preparing to lead, 152

embodying humility, 72. *See also* humility.

emotional hot buttons. *See* hot buttons.

emotional openness, 116–117

emotional Wi-Fi, 28

emotional-alert databases, 39–40

emotions. *See also* interior state of being; neuroscience; self-awareness, emotions.
disproportionate magnitude, 40
inappropriate, 40
inappropriate demonstration, 40
infectious nature of, 28
problems caused by, 40
triggering. *See* hot buttons.

energy types
deliberate choice and wise action, 2
self-protective reaction, 2

engaged in mindlessness, 17

Enron, 3

entitlement, feelings of, 103–104

ethics. *See* guiding intentions.

evoking a quality, 167–168

examples. *See* case studies and anecdotes.

explanation *versus* occurrence, 174

external reality *versus* internal, 39

facilitating meetings, personal practices, 144

facilitators. *See* fire tenders.

fact *versus* supposition, 174

failure, attitudes about, 104

faith, dealing with surprises, 106–107

farmworkers task force, anecdote, 104

fear, examples of, 44–45

federal law enforcement officers meeting, 1–2

feedback from participants, after a meeting, 184

Feeding Your Demons, 135

feelings
limiting, overcoming, 134–139
self-awareness, 39

fire
forest fire analogy, 25–26

THE ASTD MISSION:

Through exceptional learning and performance, we create a world that works better.

The American Society for Training & Development provides world-class professional development opportunities, content, networking, and resources for workplace learning and performance professionals.

Dedicated to helping members increase their relevance, enhance their skills, and align learning to business results, ASTD sets the standard for best practices within the profession.

The society is recognized for shaping global discussions on workforce development and providing the tools to demonstrate the impact of learning on the organizational bottom line. ASTD represents the profession's interests to corporate executives, policy makers, academic leaders, small business owners, and consultants through world-class content, convening opportunities, professional development, and awards and recognition.

Resources
- *T+D (Training + Development)* Magazine
- ASTD Press
- Industry Newsletters
- Research and Benchmarking
- Representation to Policy Makers

Networking
- Local Chapters
- Online Communities
- ASTD Connect
- Benchmarking Forum
- Learning Executives Network

Professional Development
- Certificate Programs
- Conferences and Workshops
- Online Learning
- CPLP™ Certification Through the ASTD Certification Institute
- Career Center and Job Bank

Awards and Best Practices
- ASTD BEST Awards
- Excellence in Practice Awards
- E-Learning Courseware Certification (ECC) Through the ASTD Certification Institute

Learn more about ASTD at www.astd.org.
1.800.628.2783 (U.S.) or 1.703.683.8100
customercare@astd.org

030615.31410

ASTD

Berrett–Koehler
Publishers

Berrett-Koehler is an independent publisher dedicated to an ambitious mission: Connecting people and ideas to create a world that works for all.

We believe that the solutions to the world's problems will come from all of us, working at all levels: in our organizations, in our society, and in our own lives. Our BK Business books help people make their organizations more humane, democratic, diverse, and effective (we don't think there's any contradiction there). Our BK Currents books offer pathways to creating a more just, equitable, and sustainable society. Our BK Life books help people create positive change in their lives and align their personal practices with their aspirations for a better world.

All of our books are designed to bring people seeking positive change together around the ideas that empower them to see and shape the world in a new way.

And we strive to practice what we preach. At the core of our approach is Stewardship, a deep sense of responsibility to administer the company for the benefit of all of our stakeholder groups including authors, customers, employees, investors, service providers, and the communities and environment around us. Everything we do is built around this and our other key values of quality, partnership, inclusion, and sustainability.

This is why we are both a B-Corporation and a California Benefit Corporation—a certification and a for-profit legal status that require us to adhere to the highest standards for corporate, social, and environmental performance.

We are grateful to our readers, authors, and other friends of the company who consider themselves to be part of the BK Community. We hope that you, too, will join us in our mission.

A BK Business Book

We hope you enjoy this BK Business book. BK Business books pioneer new leadership and management practices and socially responsible approaches to business. They are designed to provide you with groundbreaking and practical tools to transform your work and organizations while upholding the triple bottom line of people, planet, and profits. High-five!

To find out more, visit **www.bkconnection.com.**